Grammar Galaxy
Mission Manual

Red Star

Melanie Wilson, Ph.D.

GRAMMAR GALAXY Mission Manual: Red Star
Copyright © 2019 by Fun to Learn Books

ISBN: 978-0-9965703-9-8

Table of Contents

A Note to Teachers

This isn't your average language arts workbook. In fact, it is a mission manual your guardian will use to save Grammar Galaxy from the evil Gremlin. In other words, it's supposed to be fun!

You or your student should read a chapter in the *Grammar Galaxy Red Star: Adventures in Language Arts* text first. If your student prefers to have you read the text, please do so. Your student will then complete each step of the corresponding mission in this *Red Star Mission Manual*. Provide as much help in reading and completing the missions as your student requires. You have the option of allowing your student to complete some On Guard (review) sections orally. Note that the Activity sections may require your assistance.

Each step of a mission may be completed on separate days or all at once, depending on interest level and schedule. Missions are short, so students stay motivated and have time to read and write in other ways they enjoy.

Students will be asked to use vocabulary words in a sentence verbally. All vocabulary words are taken from the text. Vocabulary will improve with repeated exposure. Don't worry if your student doesn't recall word meanings. Exposure to the words is most important.

Missions marked "For Advanced Guardians Only" can be given to students who want to complete them as well as older students who are using Red Star.

When all three steps of a mission are completed, you or your student should read the Update letter. Solutions to the missions are included with the update letter for students to check their own work. If you prefer to hide the solutions from your student, you may wish to fold the Update letter over and paper clip it with the solutions inside. You may also choose to remove the letter/solutions page from the book. A paper perforator can make the removal process neater. Some parents deliver the letter in an envelope to their student and even include stickers or another small treat. You can then review the solutions together. You may wish to hide the challenge solutions at the end of each unit in the same way. **For students who need more practice with a particular skill, be sure to check the website for resources at GrammarGalaxyBooks.com/RedStar.**

Share your student's completed missions in the Grammar Guardians group on Facebook at Facebook.com/groups/GrammarGuardians or on Instagram and tag @GrammarGalaxyBooks. U.S. residents have a chance to win exclusive guardian stickers, pencils, and more.

To use *Grammar Galaxy* with more than one student, purchase a digital version of the workbook with copying rights for your family or purchase additional printed workbooks. Copying from the printed workbook is a violation of copyright. Thank you in advance for your integrity.

Have a question? Contact the author at grammargalaxybooks@gmail.com.

A Note to Students

Kirk, Luke, and Ellen English need your help guarding the galaxy. After you read an adventure in the text, you'll receive a letter from the royal English children in this Mission Manual. The letter will be followed by a three-step mission. Each step can be completed on separate days or all at once as directed by your teacher.

The On Guard section of each mission is a review of previous missions. If you don't know an answer, read the related article from *The Guidebook to Grammar Galaxy*. These articles are in the text and also accompany the mission letters.

You'll be asked to use the vocabulary words from the story in sentences you say aloud. Share your sentences with your teacher if possible. Try to use the new vocabulary words throughout the week.

Alert your teacher when you need help completing an Activity section. If you are having trouble with a particular mission, also talk to your teacher. There are other exercises and games designed to help.

Thank you for reading, writing, and completing these missions to the best of your ability to keep Grammar Galaxy strong.

Melanie Wilson

Unit I: Adventures in Literature

Mission 1: Theme

Dear fellow guardians of Grammar Galaxy,

A new theme park is giving every written work the theme "Reading is a waste of time." Father is going to have the theme park shut down. But until then, we have to label books and stories with the correct themes. You will need the information from *The Guidebook to Grammar Galaxy* on theme to help you, so we are including it with this letter.

Themes can affect what we believe, so we need to work quickly. Reading is definitely not a waste of time! Make sure you keep reading.

Sincerely,

Kirk, Luke, and Ellen English

Guardians of Grammar Galaxy

P.S. With each mission, you'll complete review questions in the On Guard section. If you don't know an answer, look for the information you need in *The Guidebook to Grammar Galaxy* entries we send you.

Theme

Theme is the meaning or message of a book, poem, or movie.

Some common themes are love conquers all; crime doesn't pay; we are our own worst enemy; we can achieve the impossible with enough effort; money is the root of all evil, and technology will destroy humanity.

Themes are the author's opinion on common subjects such as love, death, human nature, overcoming struggles, growing up, family, good vs. evil, the meaning of life, money, friendship, technology, people vs. nature, people vs. society, and war. There may be multiple themes, but there is usually a primary theme.

To discover the theme of a work, state the plot in one sentence. The plot is not the same as the theme but will give you clues about it. Remember that plot is a problem and a solution. The problem in Cinderella was her mistreatment by her stepfamily. The solution was the prince meeting and choosing her for his bride at the royal ball. So, Cinderella's plot is: A mistreated stepdaughter attends the royal ball and is chosen by the prince as his bride over her mean stepsisters.

Next, note the subject. In addition to the plot, what is the book about? Cinderella is a fairy tale and like many fairy tales is about good vs. evil. A less important subject of Cinderella is love. Many literary works cover more than one subject.

Finally, determine the author's attitude toward the problem and solution. What is the author trying to say? These answers will make the theme clearer. In Cinderella, the author seems to enjoy Cinderella's happiness at the stepfamily's expense. The author seems to be saying that good will eventually win over evil.

If you are correct about the theme, you should be able to find examples to support it. Examples will include characters' actions and quotes. In many versions of Cinderella, the girl is described as "good" and "kind." Her stepsisters are described as "ugly" and "mean." The stepfamily is shocked by the prince's choice of Cinderella as his bride. In some versions, they beg Cinderella for forgiveness. They are either sent away or forgiven, depending on the author's view of what good winning over evil looks like.

☆ Step 1: On Guard and Track Themes

On Guard. *Read each sentence. Use a highlighter to mark whether it is TRUE or FALSE.*

1. Theme is the meaning or message of a book. TRUE FALSE

2. The theme of *Grammar Galaxy* is reading is a waste of time. TRUE FALSE

3. Determining the author's attitude about the plot can help you identify the theme. TRUE FALSE

4. Literary works rarely cover more than one subject. TRUE FALSE

5. The plot is the same as the theme. TRUE FALSE

Say each of these words in a sentence. *Examples are given.*

deformity – abnormality	The squirrel's tail had a **deformity**.
agape – open	My mom's mouth was **agape** when she saw my messy room.
desecrated – damaged	My baby brother **desecrated** my birthday cake.

Track themes. *Using the form on the next page, write the themes of the books you read this year. You can download another copy of this form at GrammarGalaxyBooks.com/RedStar.*

Theme Tracker

For each book you read, write the date read, title, theme, and whether you agree with the author's viewpoint. **Remember that the theme is usually an opinion on one of these subjects:** love, death, human nature, overcoming struggles, growing up, family, good vs. evil, the meaning of life, money, friendship, technology, people vs. nature, people vs. society, or war.

Date	Book Title	Theme	Agree?

⭐ Step 2: Choose the Most Likely Theme

For each book title, highlight the letter in front of the best theme. If you haven't read the book, you can read it or search for it using a library's or book store's online catalog with your teacher's permission. Use the plot description to help you choose the theme.

1. **Where the Wild Things Are by Maurice Sendak**
   a. Parents love their children, even if they're wild
   b. Parents are mean
   c. Monsters are real
2. **Alexander and the Terrible, Horrible, No Good, Very Bad Day by Judith Viorst**
   a. Someone should be punished for bad days
   b. You're on your own in life
   c. Everyone has bad days
3. **Goodnight Moon by Margaret Wise Brown**
   a. Children should go to bed immediately
   b. Children who avoid bedtime are normal
   c. Bedrooms aren't safe for children
4. **Corduroy by Don Freeman**
   a. Don't buy an old toy
   b. Mother knows best
   c. Love isn't based on appearance
5. **The Wizard of Oz by Lyman Frank Baum**
   a. There's no place like home
   b. Dogs can survive tornadoes
   c. Magic is real

Activity. Read *Wonder* by R. J. Palacio or another book aloud as a family. Discuss the theme of the book when you've finished it.

★ Step 3: Read the Story and Determine the Theme

Read the story below and then answer the questions about the theme that follow.

"The True History of the Hare and the Tortoise"
from *Fifty-One Tales* by Lord Dunsanay

For a long time there was doubt with acrimony [hostility] among the beasts as to whether the Hare or the Tortoise could run the swifter. Some said the Hare was the swifter of the two because he had such long ears, and others said the Tortoise was the swifter because anyone whose shell was so hard as that should be able to run hard too. And lo, the forces of estrangement [hostility] and disorder perpetually postponed [kept putting off] a decisive contest.

But when there was nearly war among the beasts, at last an arrangement was come to and it was decided that the Hare and the Tortoise should run a race of five hundred yards so that all should see who was right.

"Ridiculous nonsense!" said the Hare, and it was all his backers could do to get him to run.

"The contest is most welcome to me," said the Tortoise, "I shall not shirk [avoid] it."

O, how his backers cheered.

Feeling ran high on the day of the race; the goose rushed at the fox and nearly pecked him. Both sides spoke loudly of the approaching victory up to the very moment of the race.

"I am absolutely confident of success," said the Tortoise. But the Hare said nothing; he looked bored and cross. Some of his supporters deserted him then and went to the other side, who were loudly cheering the Tortoise's inspiriting words. But many remained with the Hare.

"We shall not be disappointed in him," they said. "A beast with such long ears is bound to win."

"Run hard," said the supporters of the Tortoise.

And "run hard" became a kind of catch-phrase which everybody repeated to one another. "Hard shell and hard living. That's what the country wants. Run hard," they said. And these words were never uttered but multitudes cheered from their hearts.

Then they were off, and suddenly there was a hush.

The Hare dashed off for about a hundred yards, then he looked round to see where his rival was.

"It is rather absurd," he said, "to race with a Tortoise." And he sat down and scratched himself. "Run hard! Run hard!" shouted some.

"Let him rest," shouted others. And "let him rest" became a catch-phrase too.

And after a while his rival drew near to him.

"There comes that [terrible] Tortoise," said the Hare, and he got up and ran as hard as could be so that he should not let the Tortoise beat him.

"Those ears will win," said his friends. "Those ears will win and establish upon an incontestable footing [undeniably] the truth of what we have said." And some of them turned to the backers of the Tortoise and said: "What about your beast now?"

"Run hard," they replied. "Run hard."

14

The Hare ran on for nearly three hundred yards, nearly in fact as far as the winning-post, when it suddenly struck him what a fool he looked running races with a Tortoise who was nowhere in sight, and he sat down again and scratched.

"Run hard. Run hard," said the crowd, and "Let him rest."

"Whatever is the use of it?" said the Hare, and this time he stopped for good. Some say he slept.

There was desperate excitement for an hour or two, and then the Tortoise won.

"Run hard. Run hard," shouted his backers. "Hard shell and hard living: that's what has done it." And then they asked the Tortoise what his achievement signified, and he went and asked the Turtle. And the Turtle said, "It is a glorious victory for the forces of swiftness." And then the Tortoise repeated it to his friends. And all the beasts said nothing else for years. And even to this day, "a glorious victory for the forces of swiftness" is a catch-phrase in the house of the snail.

And the reason that this version of the race is not widely known is that very few of those that witnessed it survived the great forest-fire that happened shortly after. It came up over the weald [woods] by night with a great wind. The Hare and the Tortoise and a very few of the beasts saw it far off from a high bare hill that was at the edge of the trees, and they hurriedly called a meeting to decide what messenger they should send to warn the beasts in the forest.

They sent the Tortoise.

What is the plot (problem / solution) of the story in one sentence?

_____

_____

What is the subject of the story, or what is it really about? **Note:** *animals usually represent people.*

_____

_____

What is the author's attitude toward the problem / solution of the story?

_____

_____

What is the theme of the story?

_____

_____

What is an example that supports the theme?

_____

_____

_____

Vocabulary Victory! *What do each of these words mean? Check Step 1 if you need a reminder.*

deformity	The protagonist does indeed have a facial **deformity.**
agape	Everyone stared at her, mouths **agape**.
desecrated	Who would have **desecrated** a book this way?

☆ Advanced Guardians Only

Rewrite the Tortoise and the Hare story with a new theme. *Keep the tortoise racing the hare but change the plot to support one of these themes: love conquers all; greed is the root of all evil; technology will destroy humanity.*

Make some notes about your setting, the rising action, and the climax of the story in the chart on the next page. Then write a first draft of your story by typing it or writing it on the lines provided.

Setting	Rising Action	Climax

_____
_____
_____
_____
_____
_____
_____
_____
_____
_____
_____
_____
_____
_____
_____
_____
_____
_____
_____
_____
_____
_____

Mission 1: Update

Dear fellow guardians,

Father was able to have the theme park shut down. That's the good news. It's good news, too, that we've been able to correctly label the theme of many books. However, we think there are still books that have been marked with the wrong theme. Be looking for them and recording the themes of the books you read.

We are including the solutions to this mission.

Sincerely,

Kirk, Luke, and Ellen English

Guardians of Grammar Galaxy

P.S. This is a good time to have you sign the Guardian of the Galaxy Pledge for the year. You'll find it following the solutions.

Step 1 Solutions
On Guard.
1. Theme is the meaning or message of a book.   TRUE   FALSE
2. The theme of *Grammar Galaxy* is reading is a waste of time.   TRUE   FALSE
3. Determining the author's attitude about the plot can help you identify the theme.   TRUE   FALSE
4. Literary works rarely cover more than one subject.   TRUE   FALSE
5. The plot is the same as the theme.   TRUE   FALSE

Step 2 Solutions
1. ***Where the Wild Things Are* by Maurice Sendak**
   a. Parents love their children, even if they're wild
   b. Parents are mean
   c. Monsters are real
2. ***Alexander and the Terrible, Horrible, No Good, Very Bad Day* by Judith Viorst**
   a. Someone should be punished for bad days
   b. You're on your own in life
   c. Everyone has bad days
3. ***Goodnight Moon* by Margaret Wise Brown**
   a. Children should go to bed immediately
   b. Children who avoid bedtime are normal
   c. Bedrooms aren't safe for children
4. ***Corduroy* by Don Freeman**
   a. Don't buy an old toy
   b. Mother knows best
   c. Love isn't based on appearance
5. ***The Wizard of Oz* by Lyman Frank Baum**
   a. There's no place like home
   b. Dogs can survive tornadoes
   c. Magic is real

Step 3 Solutions – answers may vary
What is the plot (problem / solution) of the story in one sentence?
After Tortoise beats Hare in a race, he is chosen to get help for a forest fire and everyone dies.

What is the subject of the story, or what is it really about? **Note:** *animals usually represent people.*
Competition and choosing leaders

What is the author's attitude toward the problem / solution of the story?
The author thinks those who chose Tortoise to warn of the fire are fools

What is the theme of the story?
The most qualified person doesn't always win; people listen to catch-phrases or slogans more than reason

What is an example that supports the theme?
And the Turtle said, "It is a glorious victory for the forces of swiftness." And then the Tortoise repeated it to his friends. And all the beasts said nothing else for years.

Guardian of the Galaxy Pledge

I am committed to fulfilling my duties as a guardian of Grammar Galaxy, the most important of which is to read. I pledge to choose good books that I can read myself or have read to me. I will do my very best to read every day so I can learn, enjoy life, and keep the galaxy strong.

Signed,

_____

Date:_____

Mission 2: Supporting Evidence

Dear guardian friends,

Material is missing from books and articles. These sentences and paragraphs are used as supporting evidence. They help make writers' work believable and help readers understand what they're reading. The Gremlin has talked supporting evidence into going on strike. We need you to find these sentences and paragraphs and convince them to continue supporting written works.

You'll find instructions in the mission that follows. We are including the information you need from *The Guidebook to Grammar Galaxy below*. Thanks in advance for your help getting supporting evidence back to work.

Sincerely,

Kirk, Luke, and Ellen English

Guardians of Grammar Galaxy

P.S. Keep reading books and recording the themes you discover.

Supporting Evidence
Supporting evidence is what readers use to form opinions about a written work. It is also what writers use to create believable characters, plots, and arguments.
Supporting evidence includes dialogue, events, and quotes from fictional texts. In nonfiction works, supporting evidence may include statistics, graphs, quotes, and references.
Learning to identify and use supporting evidence improves reading comprehension and writing skills

⭐ Step 1: Stay On Guard & Replace Supporting Evidence

On Guard. *Read the sentence. Use a highlighter to mark TRUE or FALSE for each.*

1. The theme of Chapter 2 of *Grammar Galaxy: Red Star* is "Kids can't be trusted."   TRUE   FALSE

2. Themes are based on facts and not opinions.   TRUE   FALSE

3. If your theme is correct, you should be able to find supporting evidence for it.   TRUE   FALSE

4. Supporting evidence is only in nonfiction works.   TRUE   FALSE

5. Authors use supporting evidence to make characters believable.   TRUE   FALSE

Say each of these words in a sentence. *Examples are given.*

casualties – victims	There were no **casualties** when my pet snake got out.
reproved – criticized	My brother was **reproved** for eating with his mouth open.
condescendingly – scornfully	We shouldn't speak **condescendingly** about others' incorrect grammar.

Replace supporting evidence. *Read the selection on the mission of Spaceguard. Then number the missing sentences 1-5 to show where they belong in the passage.*

Programs that are designed to minimize the risk of NEOs are collectively called Spaceguard. Spaceguard was given a mission.

1.

2.

3.

Tracking spots NEOs years in advance of potential impact.

The goal is not to destroy NEOs. Fragments could be just as destructive.

4.

The ATLAS project focuses on NEOs that are likely to hit the planet surface.

5.

_____Once the NEOs are identified, the next step for Spaceguard is to track them.

_____The mission was to detect over 90% of NEOs with diameters over 1 km.

_____It alerts citizens of an incoming NEO and helps them leave the area of expected impact.

_____Large NEOs are the mission focus because the smallest NEOs are destroyed by the atmosphere.

_____Instead, some scientists believe spacecraft could be used to change NEO orbits.

⭐ Step 2: Highlight Supporting Evidence

Read the paragraphs below. *Highlight sentences that are supporting evidence of a widespread problem with missing sentences.*

Kirk was determined to prove to his father that what he had read was correct. He began researching GASA's NEO plan after dinner. He was pleased when he found a separate article in a different science magazine. But as he read, he found the same information missing. "Do I have to pay to read?" he muttered to himself. He didn't see anything that said the article was for subscribers only. He tried a different article, only to discover that it had missing sentences as well. *Has the plan become secret?* he wondered. *Was his father right that it was inaccurate reporting that was being changed?*

He decided to drop the research for the moment so he could finish his literature homework. His question for the first chapter of *The Bridge to Terabithia* was, "Why does Jess believe he will be the fastest runner in the fifth grade?" Kirk went to skim the first chapter of the book for the answer. He read Jess's prediction that he could be the fastest runner in the fifth grade. His eyes moved down the page. He read about Jess's sister and the cow who watched him run. He noted a paragraph about his school. But then he was startled—not by what he read—but by what he couldn't. There were gray boxes where some paragraphs once were. They were not just any paragraphs but paragraphs that held the information he needed. He had to talk to his father.

Activity. *Play a food guessing game with your teacher. Roll a die. If you roll an odd number, your teacher won't give you supporting evidence of the food you're trying to guess. If you roll an even number, you'll be given supporting evidence. For example, if you roll a 1, your teacher may say, "The weather is nice today." If you roll a 2, your teacher may say, "It's a fruit." Switch roles after you correctly guess the food and see who guesses correctly with the fewest clues.*

☆ Step 3: Find Supporting Evidence for Characterization

Read the selection from *White Fang* by Jack London. *Answer the questions that follow.*

At the fall of darkness they swung the dogs into a cluster of spruce trees on the edge of the waterway and made a camp. The coffin, at the side of the fire, served for seat and table. The wolf-dogs, clustered on the far side of the fire, snarled and bickered among themselves, but evinced no inclination to stray off into the darkness.

"Seems to me, Henry, they're stayin' remarkable close to camp," Bill commented.

Henry, squatting over the fire and settling the pot of coffee with a piece of ice, nodded. Nor did he speak till he had taken his seat on the coffin and begun to eat.

"They know where their hides is safe," he said. "They'd sooner eat grub than be grub. They're pretty wise, them dogs."

Bill shook his head. "Oh, I don't know."

His comrade looked at him curiously. "First time I ever heard you say anything about their not bein' wise."

"Henry," said the other, munching with deliberation the beans he was eating, "did you happen to notice the way them dogs kicked up when I was a-feedin' 'em?"

"They did cut up more'n usual," Henry acknowledged.

"How many dogs 've we got, Henry?"

"Six."

"Well, Henry . . ." Bill stopped for a moment, in order that his words might gain greater significance. "As I was sayin', Henry, we've got six dogs. I took six fish out of the bag. I gave one fish to each dog, an', Henry, I was one fish short."

"You counted wrong."

"We've got six dogs," the other reiterated dispassionately. "I took out six fish. One Ear didn't get no fish. I came back to the bag afterward an' got 'm his fish."

"We've only got six dogs," Henry said.

"Henry," Bill went on. "I won't say they was all dogs, but there was seven of 'm that got fish."

Henry stopped eating to glance across the fire and count the dogs.

"There's only six now," he said.

"I saw the other one run off across the snow," Bill announced with cool positiveness. "I saw seven."

Henry looked at him commiseratingly, and said, "I'll be almighty glad when this trip's over."

"What d'ye mean by that?" Bill demanded.

"I mean that this load of ourn is gettin' on your nerves, an' that you're beginnin' to see things."

"I thought of that," Bill answered gravely. "An' so, when I saw it run off across the snow, I looked in the snow an' saw its tracks. Then I counted the dogs an' there was still six of 'em. The tracks is there in the snow now. D'ye want to look at 'em? I'll show 'em to you."

Henry did not reply, but munched on in silence, until, the meal finished, he topped it with a final cup of coffee. He wiped his mouth with the back of his hand and said: "Then you're thinkin' as it was—"

A long wailing cry, fiercely sad, from somewhere in the darkness, had interrupted him. He stopped to listen to it, then he finished his sentence with a wave of his hand toward the sound of the cry, "—one of them?"

Bill nodded. "I'd a blame sight sooner think that than anything else. You noticed yourself the row the dogs made."

Cry after cry, and answering cries, were turning the silence into a bedlam. From every side the cries arose, and the dogs betrayed their fear by huddling together and so close to the fire that their hair was scorched by the heat. Bill threw on more wood, before lighting his pipe.

"I'm thinking you're down in the mouth some," Henry said.

"Henry . . ." He sucked meditatively at his pipe for some time before he went on. "Henry, I was a-thinkin' what a blame sight luckier he is than you an' me'll ever be."

He indicated the third person by a downward thrust of the thumb to the box on which they sat.

"You an' me, Henry, when we die, we'll be lucky if we get enough stones over our carcasses to keep the dogs off of us."

"But we ain't got people an' money an' all the rest, like him," Henry rejoined. "Long-distance funerals is somethin' you an' me can't exactly afford."

26

"What gets me, Henry, is what a chap like this, that's a lord or something in his own country, and that's never had to bother about grub nor blankets; why he comes a-buttin' round the Godforsaken ends of the earth—that's what I can't exactly see."

"He might have lived to a ripe old age if he'd stayed at home," Henry agreed.

Bill opened his mouth to speak, but changed his mind. Instead, he pointed towards the wall of darkness that pressed about them from every side. There was no suggestion of form in the utter blackness; only could be seen a pair of eyes gleaming like live coals. Henry indicated with his head a second pair, and a third. A circle of the gleaming eyes had drawn about their camp. Now and again a pair of eyes moved, or disappeared to appear again a moment later.

The unrest of the dogs had been increasing, and they stampeded, in a surge of sudden fear, to the near side of the fire, cringing and crawling about the legs of the men. In the scramble one of the dogs had been overturned on the edge of the fire, and it had yelped with pain and fright as the smell of its singed coat possessed the air. The commotion caused the circle of eyes to shift restlessly for a moment and even to withdraw a bit, but it settled down again as the dogs became quiet.

"Henry, it's a blame misfortune to be out of ammunition."

Bill had finished his pipe and was helping his companion to spread the bed of fur and blanket upon the spruce boughs which he had laid over the snow before supper. Henry grunted, and began unlacing his moccasins.

"How many cartridges did you say you had left?" he asked.

"Three," came the answer. "An' I wisht 'twas three hundred. Then I'd show 'em what for...!"

He shook his fist angrily at the gleaming eyes, and began securely to prop his moccasins before the fire.

"An' I wisht this cold snap'd break," he went on. "It's ben fifty below for two weeks now. An' I wisht I'd never started on this trip, Henry. I don't like the looks of it. I don't feel right, somehow. An' while I'm wishin', I wisht the trip was over an' done with, an' you an' me a-sittin' by the fire in Fort McGurry just about now an' playing cribbage—that's what I wisht."

Henry grunted and crawled into bed. As he dozed off he was aroused by his comrade's voice.

"Say, Henry, that other one that come in an' got a fish—why didn't the dogs pitch into it? That's what's botherin' me."

"You're botherin' too much, Bill," came the sleepy response. "You was never like this before. You jes' shut up now, an' go to sleep, an' you'll be all hunkydory in the mornin'. Your stomach's sour, that's what's botherin' you."

1. What is Bill nervous about?

2. What evidence is there that Henry isn't as nervous as Bill?

3. What evidence is there that Bill isn't normally this nervous?

4. What evidence is there that the dogs are nervous too?

5. What bothers Bill about the extra dog getting fish?

Vocabulary Victory! Do you remember what these words mean? *Check Step 1 if you need a reminder.*

casualties	They could cause massive damage and **casualties**.
reproved	Kirk **reproved** him.
condescendingly	"They're not going to blow them up," Kirk said **condescendingly**.

☆ <u>Advanced Guardians Only</u>

We are going to ask for brave volunteers on planet Composition. *We think words and sentences will want to be heroes more than they want to be on strike. To help us, write evidence that one of your favorite movie or book protagonists is brave. Describe the character's brave actions and include direct quotes that show bravery.*

The brave character is _____

from the book/ movie _____.

The character's brave actions include:

Direct quotes that are supporting evidence for bravery are (use quotation marks):

28

OFFICIAL GUARDIAN MAIL

Mission 2: Update

Dear brave guardians,

     Your hard work helped us talk supporting evidence into ending their strike! The gray boxes should be gone, unless we missed a few sentences and paragraphs. Please be on the lookout for them. We need supporting evidence in this galaxy. These words and paragraphs make a difference, as do you. Be sure to compare your answers to the solutions we are sending you.

Gratefully,

Kirk, Luke, and Ellen English
Guardians of Grammar Galaxy

Step 1 Solutions

On Guard.

1. The theme of Chapter 2 of *Grammar Galaxy: Red Star* is "Kids can't be trusted."	TRUE	FALSE
2. Themes are based on facts and not opinions.	TRUE	FALSE
3. If your theme is correct, you should be able to find supporting evidence for it.	TRUE	FALSE
4. Supporting evidence is only in nonfiction works.	TRUE	FALSE
5. Authors use supporting evidence to make characters believable.	TRUE	FALSE

Replace supporting evidence.

3 Once the NEOs are identified, the next step for Spaceguard is to track them.

1 The mission was to detect over 90% of NEOs with diameters over 1 km.

5 It alerts citizens of an incoming NEO and helps them leave the area of expected impact.

2 Large NEOs are the mission focus because the smallest NEOs are destroyed by the atmosphere.

4 Instead, some scientists believe spacecraft could be used to change NEO orbits.

Step 2 Solutions – answers may vary

Kirk was determined to prove to his father that what he had read was correct. He began researching GASA's NEO plan after dinner. He was pleased when he found a separate article in a different science magazine. But as he read, he found the same information missing. "Do I have to pay to read?" he muttered to himself. He didn't see anything that said the article was for subscribers only. He tried a different article, only to discover that it had missing sentences as well. *Has the plan become secret?* he wondered. *Was his father right that it was inaccurate reporting that was being changed?*

He decided to drop the research for the moment so he could finish his literature homework. His question for the first chapter of *The Bridge to Terabithia* was, "Why does Jess believe he will be the fastest runner in the fifth grade?" Kirk went to skim the first chapter of the book for the answer. He read Jess's prediction that he could be the fastest runner in the fifth grade. His eyes moved down the page. He read about Jess's sister and the cow who watched him run. He noted a paragraph about his school. But then he was startled—not by what he read—but by what he couldn't. There were gray boxes where some paragraphs once were. They were not just any paragraphs but paragraphs that held the information he needed. He had to talk to his father.

Step 3 Solutions – answers may vary

1. **What is Bill nervous about?** An extra "dog"
2. **What evidence is there that Henry isn't as nervous as Bill?** He accuses Bill of seeing things and doesn't answer when Bill insists there were seven dogs.
3. **What evidence is there that Bill isn't normally this nervous?** Henry says, "You was never like this before."
4. **What evidence is there that the dogs are nervous too?** They huddle, and later stampede close to the fire.
5. **What bothers Bill about the extra dog getting fish?** The other dogs didn't pitch into it.

Mission 3: Author Study

Dear fellow guardians,

You already know that author David Shannon missed his appearance at the library. But the problem is a lot more serious. We believe the Gremlin has been threatening authors. Now these authors are in hiding and are afraid to write.

Our father hopes that if we do author studies, we might learn enough about these missing authors that we could find where they're hiding. Then Father hopes to convince them that the Gremlin is no threat to them.

We need you to study authors by reading more than one book by them and researching their personal lives. We are including information on author studies below. Thank you in advance for working on this important mission.

Sincerely,

Kirk, Luke, and Ellen English

Guardians of Grammar Galaxy

Author Study
An author study is an investigation of an author's work and life. The study includes reading multiple books by an author to determine writing style, character types, and common themes. Biographical information and interviews connect the author's personal life to written work. Finally, an author study is an opportunity to compare and contrast personal experiences with an author's or with his or her characters'.   Author studies improve reading and critical thinking skills. They also expose readers to a variety of genres and writing styles. Author studies develop a fondness for books, authors, and fellow readers.

⭐ Step 1: Stay On Guard & Do a Biographical Study

On Guard. *Use a highlighter to mark TRUE or FALSE for each statement.*

1. Books and movies have themes, but not poems.　　　　　TRUE　　FALSE

2. One common theme is "We are our own worst enemy."　　　　　TRUE　　FALSE

3. Both readers and writers use supporting evidence.　　　　　TRUE　　FALSE

4. Supporting evidence in fiction usually includes statistics and graphs.　　　　　TRUE　　FALSE

5. Science articles require supporting evidence.　　　　　TRUE　　FALSE

Say each of these words in a sentence. *Examples are given.*

rousing – exciting	The boys played a **rousing** game of Mario Kart.
credible – believable	Mother didn't think my sister's version of my wrongdoing was **credible**.
perpetrator – wrongdoer	In fact, Mother thought my sister was the **perpetrator**.

Do a biographical study of a living author. *Have you read a fiction book you enjoyed? If the author is still living and has written more than one book (apart from a series), request another title by the author. Then research the answers to the following questions with your teacher's or librarian's help. Check GrammarGalaxyBooks.com/RedStar for resources.*

Author name_____

Birth date_____   Birth place_____

Current home_____

Books written (list at least two titles):

Using an author biography, autobiography, encyclopedia entry, or interviews with the author, list any influences of the author's personal life on the following parts of their writing.

Setting:

Theme:

Characters:

Inspiration for writing:

⭐ <u>Step 2: Read a Second Book by the Author and Compare</u>
Make notes on the setting, theme, and types of characters for the two books as you read. Review the first book by the author if necessary.

	Book 1 Title:	Book 2 Title:
Setting		
Theme		
Characters		

Activity. *Search your schoolroom or home library for more than one book written by the same author. How many authors of multiple titles did you find?*

⭐ Step 3: Compare Yourself to the Author & Characters

After reading a second book by the same author, make note of how you are similar to the author or the author's characters in the chart below.

	Author	Characters
Where you live or lived *State, country, rural, suburban, city*		
Experiences *Struggles, family type, talents*		
Personality/Traits *Shy, daring, artistic*		
Beliefs *People can be trusted; good eventually wins*		

If you were the author, where would you be hiding?_____

_____

Vocabulary Victory! Do you remember what these words mean? *Check Step 1 if you need a reminder.*

rousing	Several **rousing** stories kept the children entertained.
credible	We consider it a **credible** threat.
perpetrator	We are in the process of trying to find the **perpetrator**.

☆Advanced Guardians Only

Complete a display board about the author you've studied. *The information will make it easier for Grammar Patrol to find your author.*

Using a piece of poster board or a tri-fold board, add a picture of the author you find online, color pictures of the author's books, biographical information you found in Step 1, and pictures that represent the author's settings, themes, and characters.

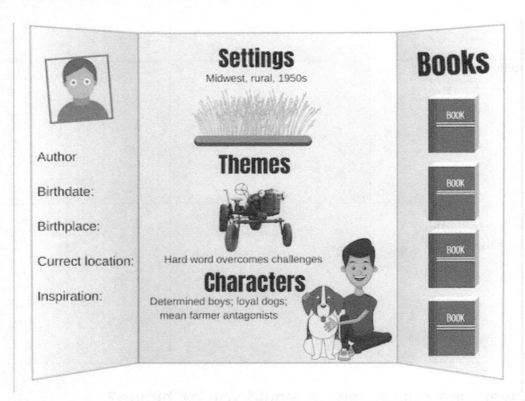

Mission 3: Update

Dear guardians,

We found David Shannon! We thought he might have returned to where he grew up (Spokane, Washington), and that's where he was. He's going to keep writing! And we found a number of other authors who were in hiding because of the Gremlin's threats. Father was able to convince them that they had nothing to fear. But there are still some missing authors. Keep doing author studies, so we can keep these writers writing.

Find the solutions to the On Guard questions on the next page.

Sincerely,

Kirk, Luke, and Ellen English

Guardians of Grammar Galaxy

<u>Step 1 Solutions</u>

On Guard.

1. Books and movies have themes, but not poems.	TRUE	FALSE
2. One common theme is "We are our own worst enemy."	TRUE	FALSE
3. Both readers and writers use supporting evidence.	TRUE	FALSE
4. Supporting evidence in fiction usually includes statistics and graphs.	TRUE	FALSE
5. Science articles require supporting evidence.	TRUE	FALSE

Mission 4: Symbolism

Dear guardian friends,

　　　Numerous words have been moved to Symbolism City where they are taking on symbolic meaning. We need your help to send some of them home.

　　　Identify symbols and their meanings. We are including information on symbolism and a list of common symbolic meanings to help you.

By the crown,

Kirk, Luke, and Ellen English

Guardians of Grammar Galaxy

Symbolism

A symbol is a setting, character, event, or object in a story that has a deeper meaning. Symbols are literal (observable) and figurative (metaphorical).

The ring in *The Lord of the Rings* symbolizes power and evil.

The lion in *The Lion, The Witch, and the Wardrobe* symbolizes power and authority.

The garden in *The Secret Garden* symbolizes a safe place.

An entire plot can be symbolic. Symbolic plots are called **allegories**. The plot of the movie *Wall-E* symbolizes saving the earth. The book *The Sneetches* by Dr. Seuss symbolizes racism.

Authors can create new symbolism in their work or rely on accepted meanings. Some commonly understood symbols are listed in the chart below.

Note that too many symbols in a literary work can make it silly.

Symbolism Chart	
SETTINGS	
Forest: often evil, the unknown	**Rainbow:** good fortune
Desert: loneliness	**Rain:** sadness
Garden: paradise or safe place	**Storms:** strong emotions
Spring: fresh start	**Lightning:** power
Winter: death	**Apple:** temptation
Dawn, light, candle: hope	**Weeds:** evil
Darkness, night: danger	**Rose:** romance
Fog: confusion	**Water:** purity
Thunder, fire: punishment	**Evergreen tree:** eternal life
COLORS	
Black: death, evil	**Blue:** peace
White: good	**Yellow:** aging
Red: emotion	**Gold:** wealth
Green: life	**Purple:** royalty
OBJECTS	
Cloak: trickery	**Circle:** perfection
Mask: demonic	**Pearl:** purity
Skull: death	**Ring:** commitment
Crown: power	**Sword:** protection
Key: answer	**Axe:** work
Heart: love	
ANIMALS	
Dove: peace	**Fox, cat:** clever
Eagle: freedom	**Peacock:** pride
Lion, bear: power	**Raven:** death
Dog: loyalty	**Owl:** wisdom
Butterfly: change	**Lamb:** gentleness

⭐ Step 1: Stay On Guard & Identify Symbolic Meanings

On Guard. *Highlight TRUE or FALSE for each statement.*

1. Theme is the meaning or message of a book.   TRUE   FALSE

2. The theme of Grammar Galaxy is "We should   TRUE   FALSE
   read regularly to succeed."

3. A character's quote may be used as supporting   TRUE   FALSE
   evidence.

4. Statistics may be used as supporting evidence.   TRUE   FALSE

5. A study of one book can be an author study.   TRUE   FALSE

Say each of these words in a sentence. *Examples are given.*

ceremoniously – grandly	The queen welcomed us to the castle **ceremoniously**.
implored – pleaded	The child **implored** his mother for a cookie.
reticence – reluctance	Her **reticence** to dive into the cold pool was obvious.

Identify words without traditional symbolic meanings. *Highlight the one word in each group of three that doesn't belong in Symbolism City.* **Hint:** *The word won't be listed in the Symbolism Chart we sent you.*

1. winter   spring   weather

2. garden   forest   house

3. candle   fire   hot

4. water   faucet   fog

5. jeans   cloak   crown

6. beautiful   white   purple

7. wealth   gold   crown

8. owl   eagle   freedom

9. peacock   lion   good

10. mask   royalty   storm

☆ Step 2: Identify Symbolism in the Story

Read the story. Highlight the words that are symbolic as given in the Symbolism Chart. *Write the meanings in the blanks that follow the paragraphs where they are listed <u>the first time only</u>.* **Hint:** <u>Use the type of symbol to help you identify it. Highlight each symbol and write its meaning only once.</u> *The first one is done for you.*

Jacob and Wilhelm Grimm. *Household Tales.*
The Harvard Classics. 1909–14.

Snow-White and Rose-Red

THERE was once a poor widow who lived in a lonely cottage. In front of the cottage was a garden wherein stood two rose-trees, one of which bore white and the other red roses. She had two children who were like the two rose-trees, and one was called Snow-white and the other Rose-red. They were as good and happy, as busy and cheerful, as ever two children in the world were, only Snow-white was more quiet and gentle than Rose-red. Rose-red liked better to run about in the meadows and fields seeking flowers and catching butterflies; but Snow-white sat at home with her mother, and helped her with her house-work, or read to her when there was nothing to do.

_____safe place_____	_____	_____
Setting	Setting	Color

_____	_____
Color	Animal

The two children were so fond of each other that they always held each other by the hand when they went out together, and when Snow-white said, "We will not leave each other," Rose-red answered, "Never so long as we live," and their mother would add, "What one has she must share with the other."

They often ran about the forest alone and gathered red berries, and no beasts did them any harm, but came close to them trustfully. The little hare would eat a cabbage-leaf out of their hands, the roe [deer] grazed by their side, the stag leapt merrily by them, and the birds sat still upon the boughs, and sang whatever they knew.

_____
Setting

No mishap overtook them; if they had stayed too late in the forest and night came on, they laid themselves down near one another upon the moss, and slept until morning came, and their mother knew this and had not distress on their account.

_____
Setting

43

Once when they had spent the night in the wood and the dawn had roused them, they saw a beautiful child in a shining white dress sitting near their bed. He got up and looked quite kindly at them, but said nothing and went away into the forest. And when they looked round they found that they had been sleeping quite close to a precipice [cliff], and would certainly have fallen into it in the darkness if they had gone only a few paces further. And their mother told them that it must have been the angel who watches over good children.

Setting	Setting

Snow-white and Rose-red kept their mother's little cottage so neat that it was a pleasure to look inside it. In the summer Rose-red took care of the house, and every morning laid a wreath of flowers by her mother's bed before she awoke, in which was a rose from each tree. In the winter Snow-white lit the fire and hung the kettle [over it]. The kettle was of copper and shone like gold, so brightly was it polished. In the evening, when the snowflakes fell, the mother said, "Go, Snow-white, and bolt the door," and then they sat round the hearth, and the mother took her spectacles and read aloud out of a large book, and the two girls listened as they sat and span. And close by them lay a lamb upon the floor, and behind them upon a perch sat a white dove with its head hidden beneath its wings.

Setting	Setting	Color

Animal	Animal

One evening, as they were thus sitting comfortably together, some one knocked at the door, as if he wished to be let in. The mother said. "Quick, Rose-red, open the door, it must be a traveller who is seeking shelter." Rose-red went and pushed back the bolt, thinking that it was a poor man, but it was not; it was a bear that stretched his broad, black head within the door.

Animal	Color

Rose-red screamed and sprang back, the lamb bleated, the dove fluttered, and Snow-white hid herself behind her mother's bed. But the bear began to speak and said, "Do not be afraid, I will do you no harm! I am half-frozen, and only want to warm myself a little beside you."

"Poor bear," said the mother, "lie down by the fire, only take care that you do not burn your coat." Then she cried, "Snow-white, Rose-red, come out, the bear will do you no harm, he means well." So they both came out, and by-and-by the lamb and dove came nearer, and were not afraid of him. The bear said, "Here, children, knock the snow out of my coat a little;" so they brought the broom and swept the bear's hide clean; and he stretched himself by the fire and growled contentedly and comfortably. It was not long before they grew quite at home, and played tricks with their clumsy guest. They tugged his hair with their hands, put their feet upon his back and rolled him about, or they took a hazel-switch and beat him, and when he growled they laughed. But the bear took it all in good part, only, when they were too rough, he called out, "Leave me alive, children, Snowy-white, Rosy-red, will you beat your lover dead?"

When it was bed-time, and the others went to bed, the mother said to the bear, "You can lie there by the hearth, and then you will be safe from the cold and the bad weather." As soon as day dawned the two children let him out, and he trotted across the snow into the forest.

Henceforth the bear came every evening at the same time, laid himself down by the hearth, and let the children amuse themselves with him as much as they liked; and they got so used to him that the doors were never fastened until their black friend had arrived.

When spring had come and all outside was green, the bear said one morning to Snow-white, "Now I must go away, and cannot come back for the whole summer."

_____   _____
        Setting   Color

"Where are you going, then, dear bear?" asked Snow-white.

"I must go into the forest and guard my treasures from the wicked dwarfs. In the winter, when the earth is frozen hard, they are obliged to stay below and cannot work their way through; but now, when the sun has thawed and warmed the earth, they break through it, and come out to pry and steal; and what once gets into their hands, and in their caves, does not easily see daylight again."

Snow-white was quite sorry for his going away, and as she unbolted the door for him, and the bear was hurrying out, he caught against the bolt and a piece of his hairy coat was torn off, and it seemed to Snow-white as if she had seen gold shining through it, but she was not sure about it. The bear ran away quickly, and was soon out of sight behind the trees.

A short time afterwards the mother sent her children into the forest to get fire-wood. There they found a big tree which lay felled on the ground, and close by the trunk something was jumping backwards and forwards in the grass, but they could not make out what it was. When they came nearer they saw a dwarf with an old withered face and a snow-white beard a yard long. The end of the beard was caught in a crevice of the tree, and the little fellow was jumping backwards and forwards like a dog tied to a rope, and did not know what to do.

_____
        Animal

He glared at the girls with his fiery red eyes and cried, "Why do you stand there? Can you not come here and help me?"

"What are you about there, little man?" asked Rose-red.

"You stupid, prying goose!" answered the dwarf; "I was going to split the tree to get a little wood for cooking. The little bit of food that one of us wants gets burnt up directly with thick logs; we do not swallow so much as you coarse, greedy folk. I had just driven the wedge safely in, and everything was going as I wished; but the wretched wood was too smooth and suddenly sprang asunder, and the tree closed so quickly that I could not pull out my beautiful white beard; so now it is tight in and I cannot get away, and the silly, sleek, milk-faced things laugh! Ugh! how odious [hateful] you are!"

45

The children tried very hard, but they could not pull the beard out, it was caught too fast. "I will run and fetch some one," said Red-rose.

"You senseless goose!" snarled the dwarf; "why should you fetch some one? You are already two too many for me; can you not think of something better?"

"Don't be too impatient," said Snow-white, "I will help you," and she pulled her scissors out of her pocket, and cut off the end of the beard.

As soon as the dwarf felt himself free he laid hold of a bag which lay amongst the roots of the tree, and which was full of gold, and lifted it up, grumbling to himself, "Uncouth [rude] people, to cut off a piece of my fine beard. Bad luck to you!" and then he swung the bag upon his back, and went off without even once looking at the children.

Some time after that Snow-white and Rose-red went to catch a dish of fish. As they came near the brook they saw something like a large grasshopper jumping towards the water, as if it were going to leap in. They ran to it and found it was the dwarf. "Where are you going?" said Rose-red; "you surely don't want to go into the water?"

_____

Setting

"I am not such a fool!" cried the dwarf; "don't you see that the accursed fish wants to pull me in?" The little man had been sitting there fishing, and unluckily the wind had twisted his beard with the fishing-line; just then a big fish bit, and the feeble [weak] creature had not the strength to pull it out; the fish kept the upper hand and pulled the dwarf towards him. He held on to all the reeds and rushes, but it was of little good, he was forced to follow the movements of the fish, and was in urgent danger of being dragged into the water.

The girls came just in time; they held him fast and tried to free his beard from the line, but all in vain, beard and line were entangled fast together. Nothing was left but to bring out the scissors and cut the beard, whereby a small part of it was lost.

When the dwarf saw that he screamed out, "Is that civil, you toad-stool, to disfigure one's face? Was it not enough to clip off the end of my beard? Now you have cut off the best part of it. I cannot let myself be seen by my people. I wish you had been made to run the soles off your shoes!" Then he took out a sack of pearls which lay in the rushes, and without saying a word more he dragged it away and disappeared behind a stone.

_____

Object

It happened that soon afterwards the mother sent the two children to the town to buy needles and thread, and laces and ribbons. The road led them across a heath [hill] upon which huge pieces of rock lay strewn here and there. Now they noticed a large bird hovering in the air, flying slowly round and round above them; it sank lower and lower, and at last settled near a rock not far off. Directly afterwards they heard a loud, piteous [pitiful] cry. They ran up and saw with horror that the eagle had seized their old acquaintance the dwarf, and was going to carry him off.

_____

Animal

46

The children, full of pity, at once took tight hold of the little man, and pulled against the eagle so long that at last he let his booty [loot] go. As soon as the dwarf had recovered from his first fright he cried with his shrill voice, "Could you not have done it more carefully? You dragged at my brown coat so that it is all torn and full of holes, you helpless clumsy creatures!" Then he took up a sack full of precious stones and slipped away again under the rock into his hole. The girls, who by this time were used to his thanklessness, went on their way and did their business in the town.

As they crossed the heath again on their way home they surprised the dwarf, who had emptied out his bag of precious stones in a clean spot, and had not thought that any one would come there so late. The evening sun shone upon the brilliant stones; they glittered and sparkled with all colours so beautifully that the children stood still and looked at them. "Why do you stand gaping there?" cried the dwarf, and his ashen-grey face became copper-red with rage. He was going on with his bad words when a loud growling was heard, and a black bear came trotting towards them out of the forest. The dwarf sprang up in a fright, but he could not get to his cave, for the bear was already close. Then in the dread of his heart he cried, "Dear Mr. Bear, spare me, I will give you all my treasures; look, the beautiful jewels lying there! Grant me my life; what do you want with such a slender little fellow as I? You would not feel me between your teeth. Come, take these two wicked girls, they are tender morsels for you, fat as young quails; for mercy's sake eat them!" The bear took no heed of his words, but gave the wicked creature a single blow with his paw, and he did not move again.

The girls had run away, but the bear called to them, "Snow-white and Rose-red, do not be afraid; wait, I will come with you." Then they knew his voice and waited, and when he came up to them suddenly his bearskin fell off, and he stood there a handsome man, clothed all in gold. "I am a King's son," he said, "and I was bewitched by that wicked dwarf, who had stolen my treasures; I have had to run about the forest as a savage bear until I was freed by his death. Now he has got his well-deserved punishment."

Snow-white was married to him, and Rose-red to his brother, and they divided between them the great treasure which the dwarf had gathered together in his cave. The old mother lived peacefully and happily with her children for many years. She took the two rose-trees with her, and they stood before her window, and every year bore the most beautiful roses, white and red.

What is the theme of Snow-White and Rose-Red?

_____

Activity. *Find five books with symbolic words in the title.*

⭐ Step 3: Guess the Symbolic Meaning

Write what you think the symbolic meaning is for each underlined word or phrase. *There may be more than one correct answer.*
Hint: *You do not have to read the book to guess.*

1. In *Alice in Wonderland*, Alice finds herself in a <u>hallway with many doors</u>.

_____

2. In *My Side of the Mountain*, Sam runs away to a <u>mountain</u> to live by himself.

_____

3. Two children use a <u>bridge</u> to enter the woods in *Bridge to Tarabithia*.

_____

4. The ghost of greedy Marley's <u>chains</u> in *A Christmas Carol*.

_____

5. The <u>journey</u> of three pets in *The Incredible Journey*.

_____

Vocabulary Victory! Do you remember what these words mean? *Check Step 1 if you need a reminder.*

ceremoniously	"We are going on a nature walk," the queen announced **ceremoniously**.
implored	"You can't reschedule?" the queen **implored**.
reticence	He hoped to make up for his earlier **reticence**.

☆ Advanced Guardians Only

Give ordinary objects symbolic meanings. *There are a number of words that would like to stay in Symbolism City. Write the symbolic meaning of these objects in your life and perhaps the words can remain in the city.*

Object	Symbolism
phone	
candy	
remote control	
blanket	
bicycle	
swimming pool	
pencil	
music	
shoes	
car	

Mission 4: Update

Dear guardians,

We sent many of the words in Symbolism City home with your help. It isn't overcrowded now, and Mother is happy we aren't being as dramatic.

You did a great job with your mission! We loved reading the symbolic meanings of many objects in your lives. We hope books symbolize fun and learning for you like they do for us.

Be sure to check the solutions we are including with this letter.

Sincerely,

Kirk, Luke, and Ellen English

Guardians of Grammar Galaxy

Step 1 Solutions

On Guard.

1.	Theme is the meaning or message of a book.	**TRUE** FALSE
2.	The theme of Grammar Galaxy is "Reading is a waste of time."	TRUE **FALSE**
3.	A character's quote may be used as supporting evidence.	**TRUE** FALSE
4.	Statistics may be used as supporting evidence.	**TRUE** FALSE
5.	A study of one book can be an author study.	TRUE **FALSE**

Identify words without traditional symbolic meanings.

1.	winter	spring	weather
2.	garden	forest	house
3.	candle	fire	hot
4.	water	faucet	fog
5.	jeans	cloak	crown
6.	beautiful	white	purple
7.	wealth	gold	crown
8.	owl	eagle	freedom
9.	peacock	lion	good
10.	mask	royalty	storm

Step 2 Solutions

THERE was once a poor widow who lived in a lonely cottage. In front of the cottage was a garden wherein stood two rose-trees, one of which bore white and the other red roses. She had two children who were like the two rose-trees, and one was called Snow-white and the other Rose-red. They were as good and happy, as busy and cheerful, as ever two children in the world were, only Snow-white was more quiet and gentle than Rose-red. Rose-red liked better to run about in the meadows and fields seeking flowers and catching butterflies; but Snow-white sat at home with her mother, and helped her with her house-work, or read to her when there was nothing to do.

safe place	romance	good
Setting	Setting	Color
emotion	change	
Color	Animal	

They often ran about the forest alone and gathered red berries, and no beasts did them any harm, but came close to them trustfully. The little hare would eat a cabbage-leaf out of their hands, the roe [deer] grazed by their side, the stag leapt merrily by them, and the birds sat still upon the boughs, and sang whatever they knew.

evil, unknown
Setting

No mishap overtook them; if they had stayed too late in the forest and night came on, they laid themselves down near one another upon the moss, and slept until morning came, and their mother knew this and had not distress on their account.

danger
Setting

Once when they had spent the night in the wood and the dawn had roused them, they saw a beautiful child in a shining white dress sitting near their bed. He got up and looked quite kindly at them, but said nothing and went away into the forest. And when they looked round they found that they had been sleeping quite close to a precipice [cliff], and would certainly have fallen into it in the darkness if they had gone only a few paces further. And their mother told them that it must have been the angel who watches over good children.

hope	danger
Setting	Setting

Snow-white and Rose-red kept their mother's little cottage so neat that it was a pleasure to look inside it. In the summer Rose-red took care of the house, and every morning laid a wreath of flowers by her mother's bed before she awoke, in which was a rose from each tree. In the winter Snow-white lit the fire and hung the kettle [over it]. The kettle was of copper and shone like gold, so brightly was it polished. In the evening, when the snowflakes fell, the mother said, "Go, Snow-white, and bolt the door," and then they sat round the hearth, and the mother took her spectacles and read aloud out of a large book, and the two girls listened as they sat and span. And close by them lay a lamb upon the floor, and behind them upon a perch sat a white dove with its head hidden beneath its wings.

52

death	punishment	wealth
Setting	Setting	Color

gentleness	peace
Animal	Animal

One evening, as they were thus sitting comfortably together, some one knocked at the door, as if he wished to be let in. The mother said. "Quick, Rose-red, open the door, it must be a traveller who is seeking shelter." Rose-red went and pushed back the bolt, thinking that it was a poor man, but it was not; it was a bear that stretched his broad, black head within the door.

power	evil, death
Animal	Color

Rose-red screamed and sprang back, the lamb bleated, the dove fluttered, and Snow-white hid herself behind her mother's bed. But the bear began to speak and said, "Do not be afraid, I will do you no harm! I am half-frozen, and only want to warm myself a little beside you."

"Poor bear," said the mother, "lie down by the fire, only take care that you do not burn your coat." Then she cried, "Snow-white, Rose-red, come out, the bear will do you no harm, he means well." So they both came out, and by-and-by the lamb and dove came nearer, and were not afraid of him. The bear said, "Here, children, knock the snow out of my coat a little;" so they brought the broom and swept the bear's hide clean; and he stretched himself by the fire and growled contentedly and comfortably. It was not long before they grew quite at home, and played tricks with their clumsy guest. They tugged his hair with their hands, put their feet upon his back and rolled him about, or they took a hazel-switch and beat him, and when he growled they laughed. But the bear took it all in good part, only, when they were too rough, he called out, "Leave me alive, children, Snowy-white, Rosy-red, will you beat your lover dead?"

When it was bed-time, and the others went to bed, the mother said to the bear, "You can lie there by the hearth, and then you will be safe from the cold and the bad weather." As soon as day dawned the two children let him out, and he trotted across the snow into the forest.

Henceforth the bear came every evening at the same time, laid himself down by the hearth, and let the children amuse themselves with him as much as they liked; and they got so used to him that the doors were never fastened until their black friend had arrived.

When spring had come and all outside was green, the bear said one morning to Snow-white, "Now I must go away, and cannot come back for the whole summer."

fresh start	life
Setting	Color

"Where are you going, then, dear bear?" asked Snow-white.

"I must go into the forest and guard my treasures from the wicked dwarfs. In the winter, when the earth is frozen hard, they are obliged to stay below and cannot work their way through; but now, when the sun has thawed and warmed the earth, they break through it, and come out to pry and steal; and what once gets into their hands, and in their caves, does not easily see daylight again."

Snow-white was quite sorry for his going away, and as she unbolted the door for him, and the bear was hurrying out, he caught against the bolt and a piece of his hairy coat was torn off, and it seemed to Snow-white as if she had seen gold shining through it, but she was not sure about it. The bear ran away quickly, and was soon out of sight behind the trees.

A short time afterwards the mother sent her children into the forest to get fire-wood. There they found a big tree which lay felled on the ground, and close by the trunk something was jumping backwards and forwards in the grass, but they could not make out what it was. When they came nearer they saw a dwarf with an old withered face and a snow-white beard a yard long. The end of the beard was caught in a crevice of the tree, and the little fellow was jumping backwards and forwards like a dog tied to a rope, and did not know what to do.

loyalty
Animal

He glared at the girls with his fiery red eyes and cried, "Why do you stand there? Can you not come here and help me?"

"What are you about there, little man?" asked Rose-red.

"You stupid, prying goose!" answered the dwarf; "I was going to split the tree to get a little wood for cooking. The little bit of food that one of us wants gets burnt up directly with thick logs; we do not swallow so much as you coarse, greedy folk. I had just driven the wedge safely in, and everything was going as I wished; but the wretched wood was too smooth and suddenly sprang asunder, and the tree closed so quickly that I could not pull out my beautiful white beard; so now it is tight in and I cannot get away, and the silly, sleek, milk-faced things laugh! Ugh! how odious [hateful] you are!"

The children tried very hard, but they could not pull the beard out, it was caught too fast. "I will run and fetch some one," said Red-rose.

"You senseless goose!" snarled the dwarf; "why should you fetch some one? You are already two too many for me; can you not think of something better?"

"Don't be too impatient," said Snow-white, "I will help you," and she pulled her scissors out of her pocket, and cut off the end of the beard.

As soon as the dwarf felt himself free he laid hold of a bag which lay amongst the roots of the tree, and which was full of gold, and lifted it up, grumbling to himself, "Uncouth [rude] people, to cut off a piece of my fine beard. Bad luck to you!" and then he swung the bag upon his back, and went off without even once looking at the children.

Some time after that Snow-white and Rose-red went to catch a dish of fish. As they came near the brook they saw something like a large grasshopper jumping towards the water, as if it were going to leap in. They ran to it and found it was the dwarf. "Where are you going?" said Rose-red; "you surely don't want to go into the water?"

53

    <u>   purity   </u>
              Setting

"I am not such a fool!" cried the dwarf; "don't you see that the accursed fish wants to pull me in?" The little man had been sitting there fishing, and unluckily the wind had twisted his beard with the fishing-line; just then a big fish bit, and the feeble [weak] creature had not the strength to pull it out; the fish kept the upper hand and pulled the dwarf towards him. He held on to all the reeds and rushes, but it was of little good, he was forced to follow the movements of the fish, and was in urgent danger of being dragged into the water.

The girls came just in time; they held him fast and tried to free his beard from the line, but all in vain, beard and line were entangled fast together. Nothing was left but to bring out the scissors and cut the beard, whereby a small part of it was lost.

When the dwarf saw that he screamed out, "Is that civil, you toad-stool, to disfigure one's face? Was it not enough to clip off the end of my beard? Now you have cut off the best part of it. I cannot let myself be seen by my people. I wish you had been made to run the soles off your shoes!" Then he took out a sack of pearls which lay in the rushes, and without saying a word more he dragged it away and disappeared behind a stone.

    <u>   purity   </u>
              Object

It happened that soon afterwards the mother sent the two children to the town to buy needles and thread, and laces and ribbons. The road led them across a heath [hill] upon which huge pieces of rock lay strewn here and there. Now they noticed a large bird hovering in the air, flying slowly round and round above them; it sank lower and lower, and at last settled near a rock not far off. Directly afterwards they heard a loud, piteous [pitiful] cry. They ran up and saw with horror that the eagle had seized their old acquaintance the dwarf, and was going to carry him off.

    <u>   freedom   </u>
              Animal

What is the theme of Snow-White and Rose-Red? Good (or love) will overcome evil.

<u>Step 3 Solutions</u>

1. In *Alice in Wonderland*, Alice finds herself in a <u>hallway with many doors</u>.
    Decisions, choices

2. In *My Side of the Mountain*, Sam runs away to a <u>mountain</u> to live by himself.
    Challenge, struggle

3. Two children use a <u>bridge</u> to enter the woods in *Bridge to Tarabithia*.
    Change, growing up

4. The ghost of greedy Marley's <u>chains</u> in *A Christmas Carol*.
    Punishment, imprisonment

5. The <u>journey</u> of three pets in *The Incredible Journey*.
    Life, hope, challenge

Mission 5: Foreshadowing

Attention galaxy guardians:

You may have noticed a shadow appearing in your movies and books. You do not have a moth or bat in your house. It's the Foreshadow. He is supposed to stay on planet Composition. But somehow, he has gotten to planet English. We think the Gremlin had something to do with that.

We need your help to send him back. Look for examples of foreshadowing in this mission so we can locate him. We are including information on foreshadowing from the guidebook. Thank you in advance for your help. Our mother is especially grateful.

Sincerely,

Kirk, Luke, and Ellen English

Guardians of Grammar Galaxy

Foreshadowing
Foreshadowing is a literary technique in which clues about future events are given at the beginning of a story. Foreshadowing builds suspense and interest in the plot. It keeps readers reading and viewers watching. Some movie genres use music to draw attention to foreshadowing.   An example of foreshadowing in the Disney film *Bambi* is Bambi's mother warning him of the danger of Man with a gun. This is a clue to his mother being killed by a hunter later in the film.

⭐ Step 1: On Guard & Identify Examples of Foreshadowing

On Guard. *Answer the following five questions or answer them for your teacher verbally.*

1. Define theme.

2. What is supporting evidence?

3. What is an author study?

4. What is a symbol?

5. What is an allegory?

Say each of these words in a sentence. *Examples are given.*

sinister – creepy	The abandoned house had a **sinister** feel.
ominous – threatening	The clouds over the pool party were **ominous**.
quest – mission	The dog's **quest** was to get leftovers.

Identify examples of foreshadowing. *Highlight Y if the example includes foreshadowing and N if it doesn't. If you aren't familiar with the book or movie, look up a plot summary with your teacher's help.*

1. In *Finding Nemo*, Nemo's father warns about the dangers of the ocean.	Y	N
2. In *Charlotte's Web*, Charlotte tells Wilbur that all things die eventually.	Y	N
3. In *The Pigeon Finds a Hot Dog*, the small bird says the hot dog needs mustard.	Y	N
4. In *The Lion King*, Mufasa says, "A king's time as a ruler rises and falls like the sun."	Y	N
5. In *The Tale of Peter Rabbit*, Peter escapes Mr. McGregor's garden and returns home exhausted.	Y	N
6. In *Click, Clack, Moo Cows That Type*, the ducks begin making requests too.	Y	N
7. In *The Incredibles*, Edna explains why she doesn't use capes in superhero suits.	Y	N
8. In *The Velveteen Rabbit*, the rabbit becomes real.	Y	N

⭐ Step 2: Use Foreshadowing to Make Predictions
Read each example of foreshadowing and highlight the most likely outcome.

But the other gnarbles warned him that he shouldn't swim so high,
As did the blyfish family that always swam close by.
"No gnarble's ever swam that high, it simply isn't done,
A blyfish might just make the trip, but we know you're not one."...
But the gnarble didn't listen and he left his friends behind.
No silly blyfish family could ever change his mind. – The Journey of the Noble Gnarble by Daniel Errico

1. The gnarble will likely:
    a. Have trouble on his trip and not succeed in swimming high
    b. Have trouble on his trip yet succeed in swimming high
    c. Have no trouble on his trip and succeed in swimming high

Wolstencroft felt sad and lonely sitting there all by himself on the shelf that was high above the Christmas cards. He longed to have a child take him home and love him and play with him. But, most of all, to hug him. For no hug is ever too big for a teddy bear. – Wolstencroft the Bear by Karen Lewis

2. Wolstencroft will likely:
    a. Never be hugged by a child
    b. Leave the shelf on his own, never to return
    c. Be purchased by a child who hugs him

Once upon a time long ago, even before the days of King Arthur, there lived a blacksmith only three feet tall...This bothered him not a bit because although he was small he was very brave. In fact, in his heart he secretly longed to become a knight and win the hand of the Princess... The littlest knight had been traveling half a day when he came upon an object in the road beneath a tree. It was a beehive. Being a kind soul he picked it up to put it back in the tree. Suddenly he heard a tiny, buzzing voice.
    We see you have kind intentions,
    But please don't put us back.
    Every knight who's seen us here,
    Raised his sword and gave a whack.
    Carry us elsewhere, we pray,
    And we'll return the favor one day. – The Littlest Knight by Carol Moore

3. The knight will likely:
    a. Get help from bees in slaying the dragon to win the princess
    b. Kill the bees to impress the princess
    c. Grow taller with the bees' help to win the princess

Activity. *Watch a mystery show or movie. Any time you see or hear something you think is a clue to future events, try to be the first to call out "Foreshadow!" Keep watching to see if you were right about the foreshadowing you identified.*

⭐ Step 3: Use Foreshadowing to Write the Predicted Outcome

Read the passage. *Identify foreshadowing and use it to write what you think will happen.*

Everyone warned him. "A pool is not the sea. You can't fish for free, it's stealing. Besides, there's all sorts of surprises in McFeeglebee's pond. Nobody knows just what is in there besides fish and old shoes and the things people lose. You'll catch something dangerous so you'd better beware. Fish in that pond? I wouldn't dare!" – <u>McFeeglebee's Pond</u> by Carol Moore

1. What do you think will happen when Georgie P. Johnson fishes in McFeeglebee's pond?

_____

_____

_____

_____

Patrick couldn't believe how lucky he was! Here was the answer to all of his problems. So he said, "Only if you do all my homework 'til the end of the semester, that's 35 days. If you do a good enough job, I could even get A's."... And true to his word, that little elf began to do Patrick's homework. Except there was one glitch. The elf didn't always know what to do and he needed help. "Help me! Help me!" he'd say. And Patrick would have to help -- in whatever way. – <u>Who Did Patrick's Homework</u> by Carol Moore

2. What kind of student will Patrick be at the end of the semester?

_____

_____

_____

_____

Vocabulary Victory! Do you remember what these words mean? *Check Step 1 if you need a reminder.*

sinister	The family was startled when some **sinister** music played behind them.
ominous	The **ominous** music played again.
quest	The Gremlin had helped him in his **quest** to leave planet Composition.

☆ <u>Advanced Guardians Only</u>
Write a letter of complaint to the editor of *The Grammar Gazette* about foreshadowing that is too obvious. Be sure to include how you feel about books and movies with foreshadowing that makes it too easy to guess the ending. We think Foreshadow will want to return to planet Composition if he knows people don't like his presence here.

Dear Editor:

_____

_____

_____

_____

_____

_____

_____

_____

_____

_____

_____

_____

_____

_____

Sincerely,

_____

Mission 5: Update

Dear guardian friends,

Thank you so much for finding examples of foreshadowing! With these clues, we were able to locate him. You did an amazing job writing letters of complaint about foreshadowing that is too obvious. We read some of them to him and he was fully convinced to return to planet Composition.

Check to be sure you have the right answers for your mission using the solutions on the next page.

Sincerely,

Kirk, Luke, and Ellen English
Guardians of Grammar Galaxy

Step 1 Solutions

On Guard. – Answers will vary.

1. Define theme. Theme is the meaning or message of a book, poem, or movie.
2. What is supporting evidence? Supporting evidence is what readers use to form opinions about a written work. It is also what writers use to create believable characters, plots, and arguments.
3. What is an author study? An author study is an investigation of an author's work and life.
4. What is a symbol? A symbol is a setting, character, event, or object in a story that has a deeper meaning.
5. What is an allegory? An allegory is when the entire plot of a work is symbolic.

Identify examples of foreshadowing.

1. In *Finding Nemo*, Nemo's father warns about the dangers of the ocean.	Y	N
2. In *Charlotte's Web*, Charlotte tells Wilbur that all things die eventually.	Y	N
3. In *The Pigeon Finds a Hot Dog*, the small bird says the hot dog needs mustard.	Y	N
4. In *The Lion King*, Mufasa says, "A king's time as a ruler rises and falls like the sun."	Y	N
5. In *The Tale of Peter Rabbit*, Peter escapes Mr. McGregor's garden and returns home exhausted.	Y	N
6. In *Click, Clack, Moo Cows That Type*, the ducks begin making requests too.	Y	N
7. In *The Incredibles*, Edna explains why she doesn't use capes in superhero suits.	Y	N
8. In *The Velveteen Rabbit*, the rabbit becomes real.	Y	N

Step 2 Solutions

1. The gnarble will likely:
a. Have trouble on his trip and not succeed in swimming high
b. Have trouble on his trip yet succeed in swimming high
c. Have no trouble on his trip and succeed in swimming high

2. Wolstencroft will likely:
a. Never be hugged by a child
b. Leave the shelf on his own, never to return
c. Be purchased by a child who hugs him

3. The knight will likely:
a. Get help from bees in slaying the dragon to win the princess
b. Kill the bees to impress the princess
c. Grow taller with the bees' help to win the princess

Step 3 Solutions

1. What do you think will happen when Georgie P. Johnson fishes in McFeeglebee's pond? He will catch something dangerous.

2. What kind of student will Patrick be at the end of the semester? A good student because he helped the elf complete his homework.

Mission 6: Flashback

Greetings, guardians!

If you are noticing that you and people you talk with keep bringing up the past, you've been experiencing flashbacks.

The first mission we had sent you was so exciting for us and...wait! We're having a flashback as we write this letter. We need your help to stop the overuse of flashback.

We are headed to planet Composition to remove unnecessary flashbacks. We need you to identify them in this mission. We're including guidebook information on flashback. We're counting on you!

To our future,

Kirk, Luke, and Ellen English

Guardians of Grammar Galaxy

Flashback
A flashback in a book or movie is an interruption of the present time with a scene from the past. Flashbacks can help explain events and characters' behavior.
Flashbacks in literature should not be overused. They do provide information. But they stop the action that keeps readers and viewers engaged. Use flashbacks sparingly, keep them short, and don't use them near the beginning of a story.
Flashbacks may be identified using the following as clues: a line break in the text, references to the past (e.g., an hour earlier), or use of the past perfect tense (e.g., She had struggled with spelling.)
Clues that the book has returned to the present include references to circumstances before the flashback (e.g., The pain in her leg disturbed her thoughts.) or use of simple past tense (e.g., She ate her eggs and asked for help adjusting her pillow).

★ Step 1: On Guard & Identify Past Verb Tense

On Guard. *Highlight a, b, or c as the best answer.*

1. "You can achieve the impossible with enough effort" is a:
   a. symbol
   b. theme
   c. author study

2. Identifying supporting evidence improves your:
   a. looks
   b. finances
   c. reading comprehension

3. An author study can help you determine an author's:
   a. writing style
   b. weight
   c. neither a nor b

4. A forest is frequently a symbol of:
   a. romance
   b. evil
   c. a fresh start

5. Foreshadowing gives clues about:
   a. the past
   b. the future
   c. the present

Say each of these words in a sentence. *Examples are given.*

rebuked – scolded	The man **rebuked** the alien for landing in his yard.
personnel – workers	The alien wanted to go to the **personnel** office at his company.
damsel – lady	When the **damsel** saw the alien, she fainted.

Identify verb tense as simple past or past perfect. *One clue to flashback is the use of past perfect tense (use of the helping verb* <u>had</u> *plus the past participle form of the verb). Highlight whether the sentence is written in simple past or past perfect tense.*

1. Luke had struggled with his spelling that morning.

   simple past   past perfect

2. Kirk placed the last piece of his model in position.

   simple past   past perfect

3. Ellen called for Comet to come to her side.

   simple past   past perfect

4. The king had wondered if making his kids guardians was the right decision.

   simple past   past perfect

5. The queen bought Cook a new dress for her birthday.

   simple past   past perfect

6. Cook had been disappointed that her father was gone on her birthday.

   simple past   past perfect

7. The queen wanted to surprise Cook with a party.

   simple past   past perfect

8. Cook had cried happy tears when everyone yelled, "Surprise!"

   simple past   past perfect

⭐ Step 2: Identify Flashback

Read the flashbacks from the chapter. Then answer the questions that follow.

"It's not good manners to say it, but I agree with Luke. People are speaking strangely today. My father had a model spaceship that he had spent hours working on. I was forbidden to touch it. But one day, I looked for him in his office and he wasn't there. I came close to the spaceship. I touched the windows ever so gently. But the model was old, and that little bit of pressure moved a window pane. When I tried to replace it, another window pane came loose. I was frantic. I asked our butler to help me find some adhesive so I could put it back together. We fixed it and he never told my father. I've always loved him for that."

1. Which sentence above is the beginning of the flashback? Highlight it.

2. Highlight the verb phrase below that suggests a flashback.

   had a   had spent   was forbidden

3. Why was the king's family confused after he told this story?

   a. He didn't tell them he was talking about the past.
   b. They had never met the king's butler.
   c. They hadn't seen the model spaceship.

Cook emerged from the kitchen to ask how the family liked the new pastry she'd prepared. When everyone agreed it was delicious, she said, "I burned my hand." The family exclaimed their sympathies as she continued. "I had wanted to bake, but Mother said I was too young to help. So when she left the kitchen, I reached into the oven. I wanted to see if the pastries were getting brown. I pulled the pan toward me and blistered my fingers. I didn't want her to know I'd disobeyed her, so I nursed them myself. I never cried."

4. Highlight the verb phrase below that suggests Cook is having a flashback.

   burned   had wanted   reached

68

5. Highlight another clue that Cook was having a flashback:
   a. Cook burned her hand
   b. Cook's mother said she was too young to help
   c. Cook never cried

Activity. *Tell a family member a story about one of your recent activities. Then without explanation, flashback and talk about a similar experience you had a long time ago. Is your family member confused? Explain that you're learning about flashback in literature.*

☆ Step 3: Rewrite a Paragraph with Flashback

Rewrite the paragraph below to make it clear the queen is having a flashback. Hint: _Consider referring to an earlier time, use of the past perfect tense, and ending with a reference to the circumstances before the flashback._

"I'll have to take the children to see them," the queen said. "I was looking at a very old book in a glass case that opened. It wasn't locked. When I lifted the lid to touch it, an alarm sounded. I was **rebuked** by the museum **personnel**. I was so embarrassed," the queen said, covering her face.

_____

_____

_____

_____

_____

_____

_____

_____

_____

_____

_____

_____

_____

Vocabulary Victory! Do you remember what these words mean? _Check Step 1 if you need a reminder._

rebuked	I was **rebuked** by the museum.
personnel	I was rebuked by the museum **personnel**.
damsel	And I would be the **damsel** in distress.

☆ Advanced Guardians Only

Write about the current and then the past experience (flashback) you shared in Step 2. *Use a line break, a reference to the past, the past perfect tense, and a mention of current circumstances at the end of the flashback, so it isn't confusing.*

_____

_____

_____

_____

_____

_____

_____

_____

_____

_____

_____

_____

_____

_____

_____

_____

_____

_____

_____

_____

_____

Mission 6: Update

Dear guardians,

We don't want to focus on the past, but you outdid yourselves on this mission. You found many examples of flashback that we then ordered removed from our books and movies. But don't worry! We didn't take all the flashbacks out. We need a little flashback to keep compositions interesting.

We are including the solutions to this mission, even though we're sure you know flashbacks well.

Sincerely,

Kirk, Luke, and Ellen English
Guardians of Grammar Galaxy

<u>Step 1 Solutions</u>

On Guard.

1. "You can achieve the impossible with enough effort" is a:
a. symbol
b. theme
c. author study

2. Identifying supporting evidence improves your:
a. looks
b. finances
c. reading comprehension

3. An author study can help you determine an author's:
a. writing style
b. weight
c. neither a nor b

4. A forest is frequently a symbol of:
a. romance
b. evil
c. a fresh start

5. Foreshadowing gives clues about:
a. the past
b. the future
c. the present

Identify verb tense as simple past or past perfect.

1. Luke had struggled with his spelling that morning.
simple past   past perfect

2. Kirk placed the last piece of his model in position.
simple past   past perfect

3. Ellen called for Comet to come to her side.
simple past   past perfect

4. The king had wondered if making his kids guardians was the right decision.
simple past   past perfect

5. The queen bought Cook a new dress for her birthday.
simple past   past perfect

6. Cook had been disappointed that her father was gone on her birthday.
simple past   past perfect

7. The queen wanted to surprise Cook with a party.
simple past   past perfect

8. Cook had cried happy tears when everyone yelled, "Surprise!"
simple past   past perfect

<u>Step 2 Solutions</u>

"It's not good manners to say it, but I agree with Luke. People are speaking strangely today. My father had a model spaceship that he had spent hours working on. I was forbidden to touch it. But one day, I looked for him in his office and he wasn't there. I came close to the spaceship. I touched the windows ever so gently. But the model was old, and that little bit of pressure moved a window pane. When I tried to replace it, another window pane came loose. I was frantic. I asked our butler to help me find some adhesive so I could put it back together. We fixed it and he never told my father. I've always loved him for that."

1. Which sentence above is the beginning of the flashback? Highlight it.
2. Highlight the verb phrase below that suggests a flashback.
     had a   had spent   was forbidden
3. Why was the king's family confused after he told this story?
     a. He didn't tell them he was talking about the past.
     b. They had never met the king's butler.
     c. They hadn't seen the model spaceship.

<u>Step 3 Solutions</u> - Answers will vary.

"I'll have to take the children to see them," the queen said. "I remember when I saw old books as a child. I had been looking at a very old book in a glass case that opened. It wasn't locked. When I lifted the lid to touch it, an alarm sounded. I was **rebuked** by the museum **personnel**. I was so embarrassed," the queen said, covering her face. She looked at the king. "I wouldn't want our kids to have a similar experience."

74

Mission 7: Hyperbole

Dear fellow guardians,

This is the most important mission we've ever sent you! It's life or death for the galaxy! Or maybe that's hyperbole?

Too many examples of hyperbole are on planet Composition and we need your help to send them back to planet Sentence. We believe that Dr. Accomplice is working with the Gremlin to label kids with hyperbole. He doesn't want them to read or do chores. If we stop reading, the whole galaxy will fall apart! That isn't hyperbole. If we stop doing chores, our homes will be destroyed! That's what Mother says anyway.

We learned that Luke has what's called Attention Deficit Hyperactivity Disorder (ADHD). He thinks fast—Luke says lightning fast!—but has some other challenges as a result. He has trouble staying focused when reading, doing homework, and cleaning. In case any of you are fast thinkers like Luke, our mother wanted us to share these tips with you.

To stay focused when you're reading and doing homework, consider: reading in a quiet place with no distractions, reading and studying for short periods using a visual timer, taking breaks that include some exercise, reading aloud instead of silently, highlighting the main points as you read, and using a bookmark to help your eyes move down the page.

Our mother also wanted us to tell you that it's easier for anyone, but especially someone with ADHD, to keep rooms clean by doing a little daily as part of a routine. She recommends making it very easy to put your belongings away, even if that means keeping things in open bins or baskets.

Please complete this mission to help reduce hyperbole. You must keep reading, and Mother says to please clean your room! It will make your parents happy.

Sincerely,

Kirk, Luke, and Ellen English

Guardians of Grammar Galaxy

P.S. We are also sending you information about hyperbole from the guidebook to help you with your mission.

Hyperbole

Hyperbole is an exaggeration or overstatement. It is used to create an emotional response in readers and listeners. *Hyper* means over, beyond, or excessive. Statements of hyperbole are not meant to be taken literally. Some examples include:

This backpack weighs a ton.
I've told you to clean your room a million times.
He was the greatest salesman who ever lived.

A little hyperbole can help readers and listeners form pictures in their minds. It can encourage them to take action. Hyperbole is used for good effect in literature, songs, speeches, and advertisements. However, hyperbole would not be appropriate in some nonfiction works like science journals.

☆ Step 1: On Guard & Identify Titles with Hyperbole

On Guard. *Highlight TRUE or FALSE for each statement.*

1. Dr. Accomplice's name is supporting evidence that he can't be trusted. TRUE FALSE

2. Watching an interview can be part of an author study. TRUE FALSE

3. A key usually symbolizes power. TRUE FALSE

4. *Foreshadowing* and *flashback* are synonyms. TRUE FALSE

5. Flashbacks stop the story action that keeps readers and viewers engaged. TRUE FALSE

Say each of these words in a sentence. *Examples are given.*

surveyed – examined	The little girl was overwhelmed when she **surveyed** the candy store.
villain – antihero	Dad complains that he's always the **villain** when he says it's bedtime.
accomplice – partner in crime	My little brother was my **accomplice** in sneaking cookies.

Identify titles with hyperbole.

Read the book titles below. Highlight the title if it contains hyperbole.

1. *Alexander and the Terrible, Horrible, No Good, Very Bad Day*

2. *The Unforgettable Guinevere St. Clair*

3. *Funny Girl: Funniest. Stories. Ever.*

4. *The Coyote Under the Table*

5. *A Mystery Bigger Than Big*

6. *A Pup Called Trouble*

7. *Forever, or a Long, Long Time*

8. *24 Hours in Nowhere*

★ Step 2: Identify Hyperbole in Sentences

Read the sentence. Highlight it only if it includes hyperbole.

1. This is the shortest sentence ever.

2. My mom will kill me when she sees my room.

3. I think this novel is hilarious.

4. The class is as boring as watching paint dry.

5. I have thousands of dollars saved.

6. My birth weight was the highest in my family.

7. My dad said my head was enormous when I was a baby.

8. It was the best match in the history of the sport.

Activity. *Look for examples of hyperbole in advertising with your teacher's help. Newspapers, magazines, radio, television, and the Internet are all good places to look. Choose a funny example and an example of hyperbole that makes you want to buy a product.*

☆ <u>Step 3: Rewrite the Sentences Without Hyperbole</u>

Read the sentence. Then rewrite it without exaggeration on the lines below.

1. It will take me two years to read this book.

_____
_____
_____

2. He owns equipment for every sport ever played.

_____
_____
_____

3. I've been killing myself trying to get my room clean.

_____
_____
_____

4. I will starve to death if dinner isn't ready soon.

_____
_____
_____

5. My sister has a million friends, and she talks to them all daily.

_____
_____
_____

Vocabulary Victory! Do you remember what these words mean? *Check Step 1 if you need a reminder.*

surveyed	She **surveyed** his bedchamber with disdain.
villain	He didn't know whether the hero had escaped the the **villain** had set for him.
accomplice	The queen arranged an appointment with Dr. **Accomplice**.

⭐ <u>Advanced Guardians Only</u>

We don't want to eliminate all hyperbole. *Rewrite the following paragraph using some hyperbole to make it more interesting.*

We have had cloudy weather for six days. It has rained several inches in that time. As a result, we have been indoors. The forecast is for more rain. We hope the sun reappears soon.

_____

_____

_____

_____

_____

_____

_____

_____

_____

_____

_____

_____

_____

_____

_____

_____

_____

_____

_____

Mission 7: Update

Dear guardians,

We were able to identify excessive hyperbole on planet Composition and send it back to planet Sentence with your help. Thank you. Is it okay if we say you're the greatest guardians ever? We don't think that's hyperbole at all.

Luke has kept his room clean all week and has been able to focus much better. He says that's not surprising because he's a genius. Now he has a new problem!

We are including the solutions to this mission. Please check carefully to make sure you completed each step correctly.

Sincerely,

Kirk, Luke, and Ellen English

Guardians of Grammar Galaxy

Step 1 Solutions

On Guard.
1. Dr. Accomplice's name is supporting evidence that he can't be trusted.   TRUE   FALSE
2. Watching an interview can be part of an author study.   TRUE   FALSE
3. A key usually symbolizes power.   TRUE   FALSE
4. *Foreshadowing* and *flashback* are synonyms.   TRUE   FALSE
5. Flashbacks stop the story action that keeps readers and viewers engaged.   TRUE   FALSE

Identify titles with hyperbole.

1. *Alexander and the Terrible, Horrible, No Good, Very Bad Day*

2. *The Unforgettable Guinevere St. Clair*

3. *Funny Girl: Funniest. Stories. Ever.*

4. *The Coyote Under the Table*

5. *A Mystery Bigger Than Big*

6. *A Pup Called Trouble*

7. *Forever, or a Long, Long Time*

8. *24 Hours in Nowhere*

Step 2 Solutions

1. This is the shortest sentence ever.

2. My mom will kill me when she sees my room.

3. I think this novel is hilarious.

4. The class is as boring as watching paint dry.

5. I have thousands of dollars saved.

6. My birth weight was the highest in my family.

7. My dad said my head was enormous when I was a baby.

8. It was the best match in the history of the sport.

Step 3 Solutions – answers will vary

1. It will take me quite a while to read this book.
2. He owns equipment for many different sports.
3. I've been working hard to get my room clean.
4. I am very hungry and want dinner soon.
5. My sister has quite a few friends, and she talks to some of them daily.

Advanced Guardians. – answers will vary

We have had cloudy weather for an eternity. It has rained buckets in that time. As a result, we have been imprisoned indoors. The forecast is for more rain. We hope the sun reappears soon.

Mission 8: Humor

Dear guardians,

We're sure you've heard about the comedy writers' strike. We are sending you a mission to help us get by until the strike is resolved. After all, seven days without a pun makes one weak. Ha ha.

In this mission you'll be reading and watching humorous books and movies you already own. We're also asking you to write new funny material. We can't wait to read your work! Find information on humor on the next page to help you.

Metaphors be with you,

Kirk, Luke, and Ellen English
Guardians of Grammar Galaxy

Humor

Humor is a device used to make people smile, laugh, and enjoy literature in all its forms. People are more likely to remember what they read, hear, or watch when humor is used. Some common ways of using humor in writing include:

Hyperbole – Overstatement makes the audience feel superior.

In the book *Kel Gilligan's Daredevil Stunt Show*, we read that Kel gets dressed by himself (without a net!).

Surprise – The reader is led to expect one conclusion when another is presented.

In the movie *Up*, Dug says, "Hey, I know a joke! A squirrel walks up to a tree and says, "I forgot to store acorns for the winter and now I am dead."

Slapstick or physical comedy – The audience feels superior to the character who fails.

Thieves in the movie *Home Alone* are repeatedly injured but not killed, making the audience laugh.

Incongruity – An unexpected pairing creates the surprise needed for humor.

In *Monster's Inc.*, monsters are afraid of children.

Irony – The audience knows something that makes the character's words or actions a mismatch.

In the movie *Toy Story*, the dialogue uses irony.

Woody: "You are a toy! You aren't the real Buzz Lightyear! You're – You're an action figure! You are a child's plaything!"

Buzz: "You are a sad, strange little man, and you have my pity."

Sarcasm – The meaning is the opposite of what is said.

In the movie *Frozen*, Olaf calls the monster 'Marshmallow' though he isn't sweet or harmless.

Pun – A joke that makes use of more than one meaning of a word.

In the book *Amelia Bedelia*, the girl is asked to draw the drapes, meaning to close them. She sketches them instead.

Overuse of puns outside of children's literature is frowned upon. Insulting jokes, including those based on stereotypes (unfounded beliefs about an entire group of people), should also be avoided.

☆ Step 1: On Guard & Read/Watch Humorous Books/Movies

On Guard. *Highlight TRUE or FALSE for each statement.*

1. Reading an author's biography can help you understand a book's theme.   TRUE   FALSE

2. Rain symbolizes good fortune.   TRUE   FALSE

3. Music can be used to draw attention to foreshadowing in movies.   TRUE   FALSE

4. Too many flashbacks can be confusing.   TRUE   FALSE

5. Hyperbole is a condition affecting geniuses.   TRUE   FALSE

Say each of these words in a sentence. *Examples are given.*

summoned – called	My dad says when he was a kid and his father **summoned** him, he answered immediately.
resolved – fixed	Mom says our argument has to be **resolved** before we can get ice cream.
subtle – understated	Our dog is **subtle** in trying to steal food.

Read/watch humorous books/movies. *Look through the books and movies you already have for humorous titles. Choose one or more to read or watch. Then write any examples you find of the following types of humor in the table below.*

Hyperbole – overstatement
Surprise – unexpected conclusion
Slapstick/Physical Comedy – failure makes audience feel superior
Incongruity – unexpected pairing
Irony – audience knows something that makes character's words/actions a mismatch
Sarcasm – opposite meaning of what is said
Pun – joke using more than one meaning of a word

⭐ Step 2: Identify the Form of Humor
Read each situation below. Highlight the humor method being used.

1. On the *Galaxy's Funniest Home Videos*: A baseball player was ready to catch the ball when he was hit in the head. The host said, "I wondered why the ball was getting bigger. Then it hit me."

   hyperbole   pun   sarcasm

2. In "Detective Robert": I didn't want to make a big deal out of her not wearing her wig, so I didn't say anything to Ms. Fleming. Instead, I took a subtle approach. At recess I gathered all the kids. Some I put on jury duty and some were the suspects. I, of course, was the judge.

   hyperbole   slapstick   sarcasm

3. In "Detective Robert": Second suspect: Jake, the class bad boy. He doesn't wash his hands before eating, he won't trade his food, and he watches PG-13 movies.

   Incongruity   pun   slapstick

4. In "Detective Robert": Last suspect: Sage. She's the teacher's pet. I don't think she did it; I just don't like her.

   hyperbole   pun   surprise

5. In "Detective Robert": That was when I decided I didn't want to be a detective anymore.

   irony   slapstick   pun

Activity. *Watch humorous home videos with and without a host making pun-filled jokes about them. Which do you prefer? See GrammarGalaxyBooks.com/RedStar for example videos.*

⭐ <u>Step 3: Write Using Each Humor Method</u>
Complete the sentences about frustration using the humor method in bold print.

1. **Hyperbole:** If I have to _____
one more time, I'm going to _____
_____.

2. **Surprise:** I get frustrated when I can't solve a math problem, when my computer is slow, and _____
_____.

3. **Slapstick:** Anne's father was worried she would drop the groceries, so he took them from her and _____
_____.

4. **Incongruity:** Joe was frustrated with his stressful job as a _____
_____.

5. **Irony:** Eli was sure his life wouldn't change much after _____
_____.

6. **Sarcasm:** Jim wasn't happy he was so tall, and his nickname of _____ didn't help.

7. **Pun:** Ally lost her pet rabbit and wasn't happy when her brother asked, "_____?"

Vocabulary Victory! Do you remember what these words mean?
Check Step 1 if you need a reminder.

summoned	The king was **summoned** by the butler.
resolved	It will eventually affect our television programming if it's not **resolved**.
subtle	Instead, I took a **subtle** approach.

90

⭐ <u>Advanced Guardians Only</u>

Write your own version of "Detective Robert," using some of the humor methods you've learned. *Make notes of changes you'll make to the characters, setting, and plot.* **Hint:** <u>*Write a first draft of the story and then add more humor*</u>*. You may type your story or write it on the lines on the next page. After you are finished with your story, check the boxes for the forms of humor you used.*

Characters	Setting	Plot

☐ hyperbole   ☐ surprise   ☐ slapstick   ☐ incongruity

☐ irony   ☐ sarcasm   ☐ pun

Title_____

Mission 8: Update

Dear guardian friends,

We are happy to report that the comedy writers' strike has ended. In fact, you had something to do with that! The writers were so worried when they saw how funny your writing was that they settled quickly. Here's one of the jokes you sent us: What do planets like to read? Comet books.

But just because the professionals are back to work, don't stop writing humor. A strike could happen again, and you might just have a career in comedy. Please see the solutions to this mission on the next page.

Laughing with you,

Kirk, Luke, and Ellen English
Guardians of Grammar Galaxy

P.S. You have finished the Literature Unit and it's time to take the Literature Challenge. Get 9 out of 10 correct and you'll be ready for an adventure in spelling and vocabulary. We recommend reviewing the information from past missions before you take the challenge.

Step 1 Solutions

On Guard.

1. Reading an author's biography can help you understand a book's theme.	TRUE	FALSE
2. Rain symbolizes good fortune.	TRUE	FALSE
3. Music can be used to draw attention to foreshadowing in movies.	TRUE	FALSE
4. Too many flashbacks can be confusing.	TRUE	FALSE
5. Hyperbole is a condition affecting geniuses.	TRUE	FALSE

Step 2 Solutions

1. On the *Galaxy's Funniest Home Videos*: A baseball player was ready to catch the ball when he was hit in the head. The host said, "I wondered why the ball was getting bigger. Then it hit me."
   hyperbole   pun   sarcasm

2. In "Detective Robert": I didn't want to make a big deal out of her not wearing her wig, so I didn't say anything to Ms. Fleming. Instead, I took a subtle approach. At recess I gathered all the kids. Some I put on jury duty and some were the suspects. I, of course, was the judge.
   hyperbole   slapstick   sarcasm

3. In "Detective Robert": Second suspect: Jake, the class bad boy. He doesn't wash his hands before eating, he won't trade his food, and he watches PG-13 movies.
   Incongruity   pun   slapstick

4. In "Detective Robert": Last suspect: Sage. She's the teacher's pet. I don't think she did it; I just don't like her.
   hyperbole   pun   surprise

5. In "Detective Robert": That was when I decided I didn't want to be a detective anymore.
   irony   slapstick   pun

Step 3 Solutions – answers will vary

1. **Hyperbole:** If I have to answer that question one more time, I'm going to lose my mind.
2. **Surprise:** I get frustrated when I can't solve a math problem, when my computer is slow, and when I don't get my $100 weekly allowance.
3. **Slapstick:** Anne's father was worried she would drop the groceries, so he took them from her and slipped and fell.
4. **Incongruity:** Joe was frustrated with his stressful job as a video game tester.
5. **Irony:** Eli was sure his life wouldn't change much after his baby brother arrived.
6. **Sarcasm:** Jim wasn't happy he was so tall, and his nickname of Shorty didn't help.
7. **Pun:** Ally lost her pet rabbit and wasn't happy when her brother asked, "Are you having a bad hare day?"

Literature Challenge 1

Carefully read all the possible answers and then *highlight the letter for the* __one__ *best answer.*

1. **If you are correct about a theme, you should be able to find:**
   a. supporting evidence
   b. an author study
   c. flashback

2. **The author's attitude about the plot will help you determine:**
   a. flashback
   b. the theme
   c. hyperbole

3. **Supporting evidence for fiction can be:**
   a. quotes
   b. events
   c. both a and b

4. **Supporting evidence for nonfiction can be:**
   a. graphs
   b. dialogue
   c. neither a and b

5. **Which symbol has the same meaning as the color black?**
   a. skull
   b. bear
   c. forest

6. **A symbol has a:**
   a. foreshadowing
   b. deeper meaning
   c. hyperbole

7. Foreshadowing in movies is sometimes emphasized by:
   a. flashback
   b. the color purple
   c. music

8. Flashback can be confusing if:
   a. it happens early
   b. it happens too often
   c. both a and b

9. Which is an example of hyperbole?
   a. It feels hot.
   b. I'm sweating.
   c. I'm burning up.

10. Hyperbole is used to:
   a. create an emotional response
   b. replace a flashback
   c. replace foreshadowing

Number Correct:_____/10

⭐ *Advanced Guardian Vocabulary Challenge*
For an extra challenge, highlight the word that belongs in each blank.

1. **My baby brother _____ my birthday cake.**
   desecrated   implored   deformity

2. **My brother was _____ for eating with his mouth open.**
   condescendingly   reproved   casualties

3. **Mother didn't think my sister's version of my wrongdoing was_____.**
   rousing   credible   perpetrator

4. **The queen welcomed us to the castle_____.**
   reticence   sinister   ceremoniously

5. **The dog's _____ was to get leftovers.**
   agape   ominous   quest

6. **When the _____ saw the alien, she fainted.**
   damsel   personnel   villain

7. **The little girl was overwhelmed when she _____ the candy store.**
   accomplice   surveyed   rebuked

8. **Mom says our argument has to be _____ before we can get ice cream.**
   resolved   summoned   subtle

Number Correct:_____/8

Literature Challenge 1 Answers
1.a; 2.b; 3.c; 4.a; 5.a; 6.b; 7.c; 8.c; 9.c; 10.a

If you got 9 or more correct, congratulations! You've earned your Literature star. You may add it to your Grammar Guardian bookmark. You can print a bookmark on cardstock with your teacher's help from GrammarGalaxyBooks.com/RedStar. You are ready for an adventure in spelling and vocabulary.

If you did not get 9 or more correct, don't worry. You have another chance. You may want to review the information in the guidebook for each story you've read so far. Then take the Literature Challenge 2. Remember to **choose the one best answer**.

Advanced Guardian Vocabulary Challenge Answers
1. desecrated
2. reproved
3. credible
4. ceremoniously
5. quest
6. damsel
7. surveyed
8. resolved

Literature Challenge 2

Carefully read all the possible answers and then highlight the letter for the **one** best answer.

1. **The meaning or message of a book is its:**
   a. supporting evidence
   b. theme
   c. hyperbole

2. **The theme of Grammar Galaxy is:**
   a. Reading is a waste of time.
   b. Reading is less important than writing.
   c. Reading is important for success.

3. **Supporting evidence can be found in:**
   a. science journals
   b. stories
   c. both a and b

4. **Supporting evidence is used by:**
   a. readers
   b. writers
   c. both a and b

5. **An author study requires:**
   a. one book by an author
   b. more than one book by an author
   c. one author interview

6. **An author study may give you which type of information on an author?**
   a. biographical
   b. scientific
   c. neither a nor b

7. **A forest is frequently a symbol of:**
   a. evil
   b. romance
   c. a fresh start

8. **Which of the following colors is a symbol for good?**
   a. purple
   b. white
   c. yellow

9. **Foreshadowing gives clues about the:**
   a. past
   b. present
   c. future

10. **"I've told you a million times." is an example of:**
    a. hyperbole
    b. symbolism
    c. flashback

Number Correct:_____/10

Literature Challenge 2 Answers
1.b; 2.c; 3.c; 4.c; 5.b; 6.a; 7.a; 8.b; 9.c; 10.a

If you got 9 or more correct, congratulations! You've earned your Literature star. You may add a star to your bookmark. You can print a bookmark on cardstock with your teacher's help from GrammarGalaxyBooks.com/RedStar.

If you did not get 9 or more correct, don't worry. Review the questions you missed with your teacher. You may want to get more practice using the resources at GrammarGalaxyBooks.com/RedStar. Your teacher can ask you other questions like the ones you missed and if you get them correct, you'll have earned your Literature star and can move on to an adventure in spelling and vocabulary.

Unit II: Adventures in Spelling & Vocabulary

OFFICIAL GUARDIAN MAIL

Mission 9: Overused Words

Dear amazing guardians,

You are literally the best helpers ever. But we do have another mission for you. You may have noticed that you are totally using the same words over and over. We are going to planet Vocabulary with our friend Cher to find out why.

While we are there, we think it would be amazing if you could complete this mission on overused words. Instead of literally using the same words over and over, use some new ones. We're including some ideas for you. We'll let you know what we learn on our trip.

Literally grateful,

Kirk, Luke, and Ellen English

Guardians of Grammar Galaxy

Overused Words
Repeating certain words in writing and speaking should be avoided. Written work can be shorter, more interesting, and better at sharing important information without these words.   Use a variety of vocabulary words instead of relying on the same few. Check a thesaurus to find better choices. A chart of some common overused words and alternatives follows.

Instead of...	Try...
amazing/awesome/great	phenomenal/spectacular/wonderful
totally	leaving it out
literally/actually/honestly/seriously	leaving them out
nice	fantastic/delightful/polite
was like	said/told
very/really	leaving them out

★ Step 1: On Guard & Highlight Overused Words

On Guard. *Highlight the correct answer for each statement.*

1. *Yellow* is symbolic for:

    hope   aging   sun

2. Clues to future events in a story are called:

    symbolism   flashback   foreshadowing

3. Flashbacks can help to explain characters':

    eye color   behavior   shoe size

4. "I'm burning up!" is an example of:

    hyperbole   symbolism   flashback

5. One way of using humor in writing is:

    author study   hyperbole   statistics

Say each of these words in a sentence. *Examples are given.*

relay – communicate	Grandma didn't have to ask us to **relay** that dessert was ready.
beverages – drinks	We laughed so hard that our **beverages** came out our noses.
trepidation – fear	My friend approached my pet snake with **trepidation**.

Highlight overused words. *Read each sentence. Highlight any overused words.*

1. The whole family agreed that Cher is an amazing friend.

2. There were totally no clues to what was wrong on planet Vocabulary.

3. There were literally no news stories that would explain the problem.

4. The king was like, "Stop using those words!"

5. He was really upset about how the family was talking.

6. The kids honestly couldn't understand why.

7. They seriously didn't want to hurt Cher's feelings by correcting her vocabulary.

8. Then they had the awesome idea of inviting Cher along to planet Vocabulary.

⭐ Step 2: Identify Replacements for Overused Words
Highlight the best replacement for the underlined word in each sentence.

1. The ladies had a <u>great</u> time watching the movie.
   wonderful   awesome   leave it out

2. Cher was <u>totally</u> impressed by the royal gardens.
   very   really   leave it out

3. The king was <u>seriously</u> upset about his family's vocabulary.
   very   honestly   leave it out

4. The king did agree that Cher was a <u>nice</u> girl.
   delightful   awesome   leave it out

5. The queen <u>totally</u> wanted to join the girls for the movie.
   really   honestly   leave it out

6. Cher thought Cook was <u>awesome</u> for making brownies.
   wonderful   polite   leave it out

7. The kids <u>were like</u>, "We can't hurt Cher's feelings by criticizing her vocabulary."
   honestly   said   leave it out

8. Cher <u>really</u> wanted to go on the planet Vocabulary trip.
   totally   seriously   leave it out

Activity. Any time someone in your family uses one of these overused words today, say an alternative back to them. Explain that you're learning about overused words.

⭐ Step 3: Rewrite Sentences without Overused Words

Each sentence includes an overused word. Rewrite it correctly. Be sure to include the quotation marks and punctuation.

1. "You have the most amazing dog!" Cher cooed.

_____

_____

2. "The groundskeepers are seriously taking care of the garden every day."

_____

_____

3. "I am literally so glad the boys weren't here to make fun of us," Ellen said.

_____

_____

4. "I totally don't think our vocabulary is that bad," Ellen said.

_____

_____

5. "Cher is a very nice girl," the king said.

_____

_____

Vocabulary Victory! Do you remember what these words mean? *Check Step 1 if you need a reminder.*

relay	The server promised to **relay** the message.
beverages	Ellen went to get popcorn and **beverages** from the kitchen.
trepidation	With some **trepidation**, the queen asked if she could invite Cook to join them.

☆ Advanced Guardians Only

Create your own overused words chart. *What other words do you and your friends use too often? What words should replace them? Or write 'leaving it out' in the Try column.*

Instead of...	Try...

110

Mission 9: Update

Dear guardians,

We have to admit that we were surprised by what we learned on planet Vocabulary. The words *amazing*, *literally*, and *totally* were behaving like mean girls. They weren't letting the other vocabulary words have a turn because they weren't as popular.

We convinced the other vocabulary words to stand up to the bullying. So, you should notice that you aren't using those three words as much. However, make sure they don't take over your vocabulary in the future!

Please compare your answers to the solutions we are including on the next page.

Sincerely,

Kirk, Luke, and Ellen English

Guardians of Grammar Galaxy

Step 1 Solutions

On Guard.

1. *Yellow is symbolic for:*
   hope   aging   sun
2. *Clues to future events in a story are called:*
   symbolism   flashback   foreshadowing
3. *Flashbacks can help to explain characters':*
   eye color   behavior   shoe size
4. *"I'm burning up!" is an example of:*
   hyperbole   symbolism   flashback
5. *One way of using humor in writing is:*
   author study   hyperbole   statistics

Highlight overused words.

1. The whole family agreed that Cher is an amazing friend.
2. There were totally no clues to what was wrong on planet Vocabulary.
3. There were literally no news stories that would explain the problem.
4. The king was like, "Stop using those words!"
5. He was really upset about how the family was talking.
6. The kids honestly couldn't understand why.
7. They seriously didn't want to hurt Cher's feelings by correcting her vocabulary.
8. Then they had the awesome idea of inviting Cher along to planet Vocabulary.

Step 2 Solutions

1. The ladies had a great time watching the movie.
   wonderful   awesome   leave it out
2. Cher was totally impressed by the royal gardens.
   very   really   leave it out
3. The king was seriously upset about his family's vocabulary.
   very   honestly   leave it out
4. The king did agree that Cher was a nice girl.
   delightful   awesome   leave it out
5. The queen totally wanted to join the girls for the movie.
   really   honestly   leave it out
6. Cher thought Cook was awesome for making brownies.
   wonderful   polite   leave it out
7. The kids were like, "We can't hurt Cher's feelings by criticizing her vocabulary."
   honestly   said   leave it out
8. Cher really wanted to go on the planet Vocabulary trip.
   totally   seriously   leave it out

Step 3 Solutions – answers will vary

1. "You have the most spectacular dog!" Cher cooed.
2. "The groundskeepers are taking care of the garden every day."
3. "I am so glad the boys weren't here to make fun of us," Ellen said.
4. "I don't think our vocabulary is that bad," Ellen said.
5. "Cher is a delightful girl," the king said.

Mission 10: Slang

Dear groovy guardians,

     Do your grandparents ever say things you don't understand? They might be using slang. We are sending you this mission to help you understand slang better. Check out the info on the next page.

     We'd also like you to teach your parents slang they don't know. Can you dig it?

Gotta boogie,

Kirk, Luke, and Ellen English

Guardians of Grammar Galaxy

Slang

Slang is informal, usually spoken, language used by a particular group of people. It is used to help group members feel connected by assigning new meanings to words that only they understand. Slang includes acronyms used by a group.

Youth create slang to demonstrate separateness from their parents' generation. For example, young Western women in the 1920s called new things they liked "the cat's pajamas." See the chart below for common slang from previous generations.

Jargon is a form of slang often used within professional groups. For example, the term *pro se* (for someone who represents himself or herself in court without a lawyer) is legal jargon.

Portmanteau slang is a slang word that is a combination of two words. (A portmanteau is a suitcase that opens like a book with a container on each side.) For example, *ginormous* is portmanteau slang. It is from *gigantic* and *enormous*, meaning huge. *Frenemy* is portmanteau slang for someone who is both a friend and enemy.

To be certain of the meaning of slang, consult a slang dictionary.

Slang	Meaning
Far out	Fantastic
Wallflower	A shy person
Don't have a cow	Calm down
Ride	Car
A gas	Good time
Lay it on me	Tell me
Give me some skin	Shake hands or high-five
Gimme some sugar	Kiss me
Heavy	Serious
Foxy	Gorgeous
Old lady	Wife/girlfriend
Hang loose	Relaxing
Can you dig it?	Do you understand?
Groovy	Wonderful

⭐ <u>Step 1: On Guard & Match Slang to Its Meaning</u>

On Guard. *Answer the questions or answer them verbally for your teacher.*

1. What is foreshadowing?

2. What is a flashback?

3. What is hyperbole?

4. What is a pun?

5. What overused words do you use?

Say each of these words in a sentence. *Examples are given.*

ornate – fancy	I'm in trouble because I broke an **ornate** vase.
adorned – decorated	My dog's fur is **adorned** with leaves from her run through the pile.
adjoining – connected	We will have **adjoining** rooms in the hotel.

Match slang to its meaning. *Draw a line from slang to its meaning.*

far out	good time
gimme some sugar	calm down
heavy	car
foxy	friend and enemy
don't have a cow	fantastic
ride	serious
Can you dig it?	kiss me
a gas	gorgeous
hang loose	relaxing
frenemy	Do you understand?

116

⭐ <u>Step 2: Use a Dictionary to Look Up Slang Meanings</u>
Look up the underlined word or phrase in a dictionary. *Write the meaning of the underlined word or phrase on the line below.*
Hint: *<u>If your dictionary doesn't include the meaning, get your teacher's help to look up the words online or use the links at GrammarGalaxyBooks.com/RedStar</u>.*

1. The queen gave her father <u>props</u> for getting around so well.

_____

2. The queen thought Luke had had enough sugar. <u>As if</u>!

_____

3. The king thought the trail on the property was <u>the bee's knees</u>.

_____

4. Kirk was <u>bugging out</u> over a possible gas leak.

_____

5. Some royal family members have suffered from <u>affluenza</u>.

_____

Activity. *Today, use as many of the old slang expressions we sent with your family as you can. Be sure to explain that you're learning about slang. Ask the adults in your family to teach you their generation's slang and jargon they know from their work.*

117

⭐ <u>Step 3: Rewrite the Sentences Without Jargon</u>
Look up the meaning of the jargon in the sentences below with your teacher's help. *Then rewrite the sentences without the jargon, so the meaning is clear.*

1. Whenever the king got angry, the queen worried about his <u>BP</u>.

   _____

   _____

2. The king said his father-in-law was getting a lot of <u>bang for the buck</u> at his new apartment.

   _____

   _____

3. The queen checked her father's <u>scripts</u> while she was there.

   _____

   _____

4. She reordered one of them to be delivered <u>stat</u>.

   _____

   _____

5. The queen said there was no <u>magic bullet</u> for her father.

   _____

   _____

Vocabulary Victory! Do you remember what these words mean? *Check Step 1 if you need a reminder.*

ornate	**Ornate** chandeliers hung from the ceiling.
adorned	Fresh-floral centerpieces **adorned** the cloth-covered tables.
adjoining	He rolled his wheelchair in the direction of the **adjoining** hallway.

☆ <u>Advanced Guardians Only</u>
Create your own slang dictionary. *Write the slang you use (including jargon, acronyms, and portmanteau) and its meaning.*

Slang	Meaning

Mission 10: Update

Dear solid guardians,

      We have been learning a lot of slang and we know you have too. We'd like to teach you one last example of jargon that might help you as you review your mission answers. We call guardians' mistakes *gremlins*. We think of our mistakes as the Gremlin getting the best of us. While he may win a few points in our mistakes, we know that we are winning the war.

      Look for any gremlins in your mission using the solutions on the next page and rock on!

Onward and upward,

Kirk, Luke, and Ellen English
Guardians of Grammar Galaxy

Step 1 Solutions

On Guard.

1. **What is foreshadowing?** Foreshadowing is a literary technique in which clues about future events are given at the beginning of a story.

2. **What is a flashback?** A flashback in a book or movie is an interruption of the present time with a scene from the past.

3. **What is hyperbole?** Hyperbole is an exaggeration or overstatement.

4. **What is a pun?** A joke that makes use of more than one meaning of a word.

Match slang to its meaning.

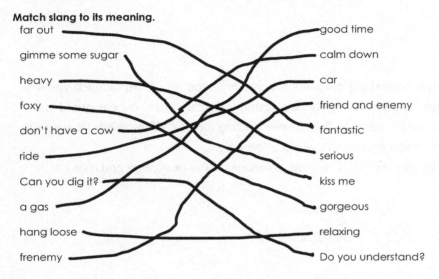

far out — good time
gimme some sugar — calm down
heavy — car
foxy — friend and enemy
don't have a cow — fantastic
ride — serious
Can you dig it? — kiss me
a gas — gorgeous
hang loose — relaxing
frenemy — Do you understand?

Step 2 Solutions

1. The queen gave her father <u>respect</u> for getting around so well.
2. The queen thought Luke had had enough sugar. <u>As if that was true</u>!
3. The king thought the trail on the property was <u>excellent</u>.
4. Kirk was <u>freaking out</u> over a possible gas leak.
5. Some royal family members have suffered from <u>excessive wealth</u>.

Step 3 Solutions

1. Whenever the king got angry, the queen worried about his <u>blood pressure</u>.
2. The king said his father-in-law was getting <u>a lot for his money</u> at his new apartment.
3. The queen checked her father's <u>prescriptions</u> while she was there.
4. She reordered one of them to be delivered <u>immediately</u>.
5. The queen said there was no <u>easy fix</u> for her father.

Mission 11: Word Analogies

Dear guardian friends,

     Mistakes are to the Gremlin as solutions are to rocks. We know that isn't right, but we had to show you why we need your help. Our mother is going to pretend to be Dr. Wordlove on planet Vocabulary. She wants to put the right words together to form analogies. That's where you come in. In this mission, you'll be learning logic and helping us match words to form correct analogies. When we can solve analogies, our thinking skills will improve, and we'll get better scores on standardized tests. We know you'll take to this mission as a duck to space. You know what we mean.

Sincerely,

Kirk, Luke, and Ellen English

Guardians of Grammar Galaxy

P.S. Check out the information on word analogies on the next page.

Word Analogies

Word analogies, or verbal analogies, are often included in standardized tests. Solving word analogies, or determining the relationship between words, is a test of vocabulary and logic or reasoning. Verbal analogies are written in this format:

up:down::fast:slow

This analogy is read as "Up is to down as fast is to slow."

To determine a missing word in an analogy, determine the relationship between the first word pair. Then apply that relationship to the second set of words. Choose the most likely word for the blank.

Rug:floor::painting:_____

In this analogy, we determine that the floor is where a rug is placed. To complete the analogy, we ask where a painting is placed. The answer is *wall*.

⭐ Step 1: On Guard & Solve Language Arts Analogies

On Guard. *Highlight the correct answer.*

1. A movie told in chronological order will not have:
   flashback   foreshadowing   hyperbole

2. "I'll die if I have to do math" is an example of:
   symbolism   hyperbole   jargon

3. Slapstick comedy is:
   emotional   intellectual   physical

4. Which of these words is overused?
   nice   phenomenal   wonderful

5. Which of these words could be considered slang?
   heavy   beautiful   slight

Say each of these words in a sentence. *Examples are given.*

fuming – furious	My sister was **fuming** because I ate the last cookie.
lad – boy	It drives my brother nuts when I call him a wee **lad**.
snide – sarcastic	Our mother tells us it's rude to make **snide** comments.

Solve language arts analogies. Highlight the word that belongs in the blank to complete the analogy.

1. **Fiction** is to **novel** as **nonfiction** is to _____.
   fairy tale   myth   encyclopedia

2. **Noun** is to **subject** as **verb** is to _____.
   adjective   adverb   predicate

3. **Desecrated** is to **destroyed** as **resolved** is to _____.
   fixed   broken   wrecked

4. **Phonics** is to **spelling** as **reading** is to _____.
   exercising   eating   vocabulary

5. **Topic sentence** is to **paragraph** as **capital letter** is to _____.
   sentence   period   comma

6. **Slowly** is to **adverb** as **over** is to _____.
   noun   adjective   preposition

7. **Side** is to **sighed** as **break** is to _____.
   broke   broken   brake

8. **Give** is to **have given** as **bring** is to **have** _____.
   bring   brought   brang

⭐ Step 2: Complete the Space Analogies

Highlight the word that belongs in the blank to solve the analogy.

Use an encyclopedia or dictionary to get definitions of terms you don't know. Ask your teacher if you'd like to search online.

1. **sun:solar system::star:**_____

   moon   constellation   comet

2. **moon:lunar::sun:**_____

   meteor   solar   penumbra

3. **biology:biologist::stars:**_____

   astrologist   starologist   astronomer

4. **Earth:populated::Venus:**_____

   uninhabitable   colonized   acclimatized

5. **gravitation:weightlessness::propel:**_____

   launch   inertia   rotate

6. **Jupiter:planet::Orion:**_____

   moon   star   constellation

7. **Earth:terrestrial::sky:**_____

   celestial   space   galactic

8. **Milky Way:galaxy::Electra:**_____

   star   comet   planet

Activity. *Communicate using analogies with your family today. For example, instead of simply asking for milk, you might say, "Chicken is to egg as cow is to?" If the answer is milk, say, "Please pass it." Be sure to explain that you're learning about analogies.*

⭐ Step 3: Write the Words to Solve the Analogies

Write the word that belongs in the blank. *Use your knowledge from previous missions (or review them) to solve the analogies.*

1. **heavy:serious::foxy:** _____

2. **hyperbole:subtle::expected:** _____

3. **wonder:had wondered::wish:** _____

4. **past:flashback::future:** _____

5. **romance:rose::good fortune:** _____

6. **death:winter::fresh start:** _____

7. **trips and falls:slapstick:: Never trust atoms; they make up everything.:** _____

8. *White Fang*:**Jack London::***Grammar Galaxy*: _____

_____

Vocabulary Victory! Do you remember what these words mean? *Check Step 1 if you need a reminder.*

fuming	He went to his bedchamber **fuming**.
lad	"Poor **lad**," Cook said.
adjoining	"Because it wouldn't look good?" the king asked in a **snide** tone.

☆ Advanced Guardians Only

Write your own analogies. *Make them for your home and see if your family can solve them. Leave the last line in each set of four blank.*

_____ : _____ ::

_____ : _____

_____ : _____ ::

_____ : _____

_____ : _____ ::

_____ : _____

_____ : _____ ::

_____ : _____

_____ : _____ ::

_____ : _____

OFFICIAL GUARDIAN MAIL

Mission 11: Update

Dear guardians,

You took to your word analogies mission like ducks to water! And like mistakes are to the Gremlin, solutions are to guardians like you.

Mother had so much fun playing Dr. Wordlove. The words accepted their new, better matches from her without complaint.

Keep doing analogies to keep your thinking skills sharp. Check the solutions to this mission to make sure we didn't miss any bad matches.

Gratefully,

Kirk, Luke, and Ellen English
Guardians of Grammar Galaxy

Step 1 Solutions

On Guard.

1. A movie told in chronological order will not have:
   flashback   foreshadowing   hyperbole
2. "I'll die if I have to do math" is an example of:
   symbolism   hyperbole   jargon
3. Slapstick comedy is:
   emotional   intellectual   physical
4. Which of these words is overused?
   nice   phenomenal   wonderful
5. Which of these words could be considered slang?
   heavy   beautiful   slight

Solve language arts analogies.

1. **Fiction** is to **novel** as **nonfiction** is to _____.
      fairy tale   myth   encyclopedia
2. **Noun** is to **subject** as **verb** is to _____.
      adjective   adverb   predicate
3. **Desecrated** is to **destroyed** as **resolved** is to _____.
      fixed   broken   wrecked
4. **Phonics** is to **spelling** as **reading** is to _____.
      exercising   eating   vocabulary
5. **Topic sentence** is to **paragraph** as **capital letter** is to _____.
      sentence   period   comma
6. **Slowly** is to **adverb** as **over** is to _____.
      noun   adjective   preposition
7. **Side** is to **sighed** as **break** is to _____.
      broke   broken   brake
8. **Give** is to **have given** as **bring** is to **have** _____.
      bring   brought   brang

Step 2 Solutions

1. **sun:solar system::star:**_____
   moon   constellation   comet
2. **moon:lunar::sun:**_____
   meteor   solar   penumbra
3. **biology:biologist::stars:**_____
   astrologist   starologist   astronomer
4. **Earth:populated::Venus:**_____
   uninhabitable   colonized   acclimatized
5. **gravitation:weightlessness::propel:**_____
   launch   inertia   rotate
6. **Jupiter:planet::Orion:**_____
   moon   star   constellation
7. **Earth:terrestrial::sky:**_____
   celestial   space   galactic
8. **Milky Way:galaxy::Electra:**_____
   star   comet   planet

Step 3 Solutions

1. heavy:serious::foxy: gorgeous
2. hyperbole:subtle::expected: surprise or unexpected
3. wonder:had wondered::wish: had wished
4. past:flashback::future: foreshadowing
5. romance:rose::good fortune: rainbow
6. death:winter::fresh start: spring
7. trips and falls:slapstick:: Never trust atoms; they make up everything.: pun
8. *White Fang*:Jack London::*Grammar Galaxy*: Melanie Wilson

Mission 12: Prefixes, Suffixes & Root Words

Dear guardians,

We hate to interrupt your holiday celebration, but we are in crisis. The Gremlin has recruited a number of prefixes, suffixes, and root words to cause trouble. See the list on the next page. Have you ever heard the saying, "Know thy enemy?" That's what this mission is all about. We have to know these vocabulary citizens well, so we can keep them from ruining our year-end celebration.

We would be so grateful if you would take some time to complete this mission. If we work together, we can resolve the crisis quickly.

Gratefully,

Kirk, Luke, and Ellen English

Guardians of Grammar Galaxy

Prefixes	Definition	Examples
anti-	against, opposite	antivirus, antibiotic
en-, em-	to cause, to put or go into	enable, embark
centi-	hundred	centimeter, centipede
deca-, deci	ten	decade, decimal
fore-	before	forewarned, foreword
milli-, mille- kilo-	thousand	millimeter, millennium, kilogram
multi-, poly-	many	multiple, polygon
semi-	half	semicolon, semicircle
sub-	under, below, secondary	submerge, substandard

Suffixes	Definition	Examples
-able, -ible	can be done	likable, sensible
-an	having skill, relating or belonging to	electrician, American
-ance, -ence	act, condition	excellence, importance
-ive	like, likely to act	sensitive, active

Roots	Definition	Examples
ject	throw	projectile, inject
jur, juris	judge, law	jury, jurisdiction
mit	send	transmit, admit
path	feel, suffer, disease	sympathy, pathology
struct	build	construct, instruct

⭐ Step 1: On Guard & Match Word Parts to Meanings

On Guard. *Highlight the correct answer.*

1. Hyperbole isn't appropriate in:
   ads   songs   science journals

2. An unexpected pairing like monsters afraid of kids is:
   incongruity   sarcasm   hyperbole

3. Instead of the word *totally*:
   spectacular   fantastic   leave it out

4. The word *ginormous* is:
   portmanteau slang   jargon   an analogy

5. **High:low::chimney:sidewalk** is a/an:
   slang   analogy   hyperbole

Say each of these words in a sentence. *Examples are given.*

mused – thought	She **mused** about what she would eat if she owned a candy store.
splurge – spend a lot	He wanted to **splurge** on a large Lego set.
intently – closely	The cat watched the moth **intently**.

Match word parts to meanings. *Draw a line from the word part on the left to its meaning on the right.*

path	under, below, secondary
-ive	throw
-ance	like, likely to act
-ject	act, condition
struct	build
sub-	before
fore-	feel, suffer, disease
-ible	send
mit	half
semi-	can be done

⭐ Step 2: Find the Words That Include the Prefixes, Suffixes, and Root Words You Learned

Read the sentence. *Highlight the word or words that include a word part on the list we sent you.*

1. Kirk thought he needed to create an antivirus program.

2. The galaxy was getting ready to celebrate a new millennium.

3. The king believes that being forewarned is forearmed.

4. The king doesn't allow subpar performance in his employees.

5. The king believes crafting a sensible security plan is the key to excellence.

6. The king didn't object to the programmer's plan.

7. Kirk admitted that he hadn't obeyed his father's instructions.

8. His father sympathized with Kirk's desire to learn from semiprofessional programmers.

Activity. *Count how many of this mission's prefixes, suffixes, and root words appear in two pages of a book you're reading.*

☆ Step 3: Guess the Word Meanings

Write what you think the underlined word means based on your knowledge of prefixes, suffixes, and root words. Then check the dictionary and write its definition of the underlined word.

1. Kirk had to have a dose of <u>antivenin</u> after a snake bite.
Guess:_____
Dictionary:_____

2. The queen once served as a <u>juror</u> for two weeks.
Guess:_____
Dictionary:_____

3. Kirk could <u>empathize</u> with his friend's disappointment.
Guess:_____
Dictionary:_____

4. The <u>trajectory</u> of the arrow looked to be off target.
Guess:_____
Dictionary:_____

5. The company sent the king an envelope for his <u>remittance</u>.
Guess:_____
Dictionary:_____

Vocabulary Victory! Do you remember what these words mean? *Check Step 1 if you need a reminder.*

mused	"We ought to have a galaxy-wide celebration," she **mused** aloud.
splurge	We should **splurge** on such an important occasion.
intently	The programmer nodded and listened **intently**.

☆ <u>Advanced Guardians Only</u>

Write an announcement that will get the warring words to surrender. *Remind them that we need their help to have a strong galaxy. Using as many of the prefixes, suffixes, and root words as you can will give us better results. Find words for your announcement in a dictionary or with an online search with your teachers help. Search for "words that include_____."*

Attention citizens of planet Vocabulary: We bring you this important announcement.

_____

_____

_____

_____

_____

_____

_____

_____

_____

_____

_____

_____

_____

_____

_____

_____

_____

_____

_____

_____

_____

140

Mission 12: Update

Dear guardians,

    We are so thankful that you worked to turn around what could have been a disaster. The prefixes, suffixes, and root words knew they were overpowered and outnumbered with you guardians doing your job. When we gave your announcements that featured them, they knew they were needed and surrendered. We can get on with the celebration!

    If you have a moment, make sure you didn't overlook anything in your mission. Find the solutions on the next page.

Cheers,

Kirk, Luke, and Ellen English
Guardians of Grammar Galaxy

Step 1 Solutions

On Guard.

1. Hyperbole isn't appropriate in:
   ads   songs   science journals
2. An unexpected pairing like monsters afraid of kids is:
   incongruity   sarcasm   hyperbole
3. Instead of the word *totally*:
   spectacular   fantastic   leave it out
4. The word *ginormous* is:
   portmanteau slang   jargon   an analogy
5. **High:low::chimney:sidewalk** is a/an:
   slang   analogy   hyperbole

Match word parts to meanings.

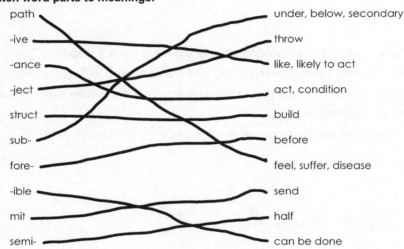

Step 2 Solutions

1. Kirk thought he needed to create an antivirus program.
2. The galaxy was getting ready to celebrate a new millennium.
3. The king believes that being forewarned is forearmed.
4. The king doesn't allow subpar performance in his employees.
5. The king believes crafting a sensible security plan is the key to excellence.
6. The king didn't object to the programmer's plan.
7. Kirk admitted that he hadn't obeyed his father's instructions.
8. His father sympathized with Kirk's desire to learn from semiprofessional programmers.

Step 3 Solutions

1. Kirk had to have a dose of antivenin after a snake bite.
Dictionary: antiserum treatment for venom

2. The queen once served as a juror for two weeks.
Dictionary: member of a jury

3. Kirk could empathize with his friend's disappointment.
Dictionary: understand feelings

4. The trajectory of the arrow looked to be off target.
Dictionary: path of flying object

5. The company sent the king an envelope for his remittance.
Dictionary: sent payment

142

OFFICIAL GUARDIAN MAIL

Mission 13: Apostrophes

Dear guardians,

We dont (do not) know if youve (you have) heard about the Impostor Apostrophe Crisis, so well (we will) tell you whats (what is) happening. Apostrophes on planet Spelling are being held in detainment camps and will be removed from the planet. You may notice that even now we are unable to use them. We have to write out contractions. Spelling without apostrophes will cause confusion.

We are on our way to planet Spelling to release the apostrophes. Thats (that is) where you come in. We need you to tell us where these apostrophes belong. Please review the information on apostrophes on the next page. Thank you in advance for being punctuation defenders.

Sincerely,

Kirk, Luke, and Ellen English
Guardians of Grammar Galaxy

Apostrophes

An apostrophe is a punctuation mark (') used to show possession, omission of letters as in contractions, or the plural of letters and numbers.

Apostrophes are used after the noun that possesses something. If a plural noun ends in s, the apostrophe follows the s.

The dog's mouth was covered in mud. – *correct*

Two dog's owners picked up their pets from the groomer. – *incorrect*; the apostrophe goes after the s.

Its, his, hers, ours, and yours are possessive pronouns that end in s. They do not use apostrophes.

Its wounded paw caused the dog to limp. – *correct*

The purse left in the café was her's. – *incorrect*

Apostrophes are used to form contractions or to indicate missing letters or numbers.

It's time to go! – *correct*; the apostrophe stands for the *i* in *it is.*

Your going to be late. – *incorrect*; use *you're* which stands for you are.

Life was much different in the '50s. – *correct*; the apostrophe takes the place of 19 in 1950s.

An apostrophe and an s form the plural for single letters and numbers. Apostrophes with an s do not form other plurals.

Does anyone have any 5's? – *correct*

Be sure to dot your is and cross your ts. – *incorrect*

My mother is having lunch with other mom's. – *incorrect*

⭐ Step 1: On Guard & Highlight Words Requiring Apostrophes

On Guard. *Highlight the correct answer.*

1. A common humor method is:
   surprise   analogy

2. The following is an overused word:
   told   actually

3. What is slang for a shy person?
   wallflower   ride

4. Solve the analogy. **day:night::bees:_____**
   butterflies   fireflies

5. Which prefix means *many*?
   poly-   deca-

Say each of these words in a sentence. *Examples are given.*

evicted – removed	I **evicted** my sister from my room, even though it's her room too.
crimson – red	I cut my finger and it quickly turned **crimson**.
ushered – guided	My mother ushered my brother out of the store because he was screaming.

Highlight words requiring apostrophes. *Read each sentence.*
Highlight the word or words in each that needs an apostrophe.

1. The kings temper got the best of him because of the crisis.

2. The kids stomachs were rumbling without breakfast.

3. "Its preposterous," the king roared.

4. "Youre going to have more confusion on the planet," he said.

5. "I know well make things right," the queen said.

6. "I havent seen anything like this since the 60s," the king said.

7. "Youll still have to mind your ps and qs," the queen said.

8. "Do you have any 5s I could have as cash?" Luke asked.

⭐ Step 2: Remove Incorrect Apostrophes

Read each sentence. *Using correction fluid or a white pen, remove apostrophes that don't belong.* **Hint:** *Some sentences may have no incorrect apostrophes.*

1. The queen realized the sweater Ellen was wearing was her's.

2. "It's a sad day when punctuation is detained," the king said.

3. Planet Spelling can't be left to it's own any longer.

4. The apostrophes' were being transported elsewhere.

5. "Be sure to bring you'r communicators," the king instructed.

6. "If you don't leave now, you'll risk apostrophe's being recycled."

7. "Remember that you're not going to see the A's."

8. "And you shouldn't stop to see any show's."

Activity. *Apostrophes are frequently misused. This week look for incorrect use of apostrophes (missing or added when they shouldn't be) and tell your teacher when you find examples.*

☆ Step 3: Write the Sentences Using Apostrophes Correctly

Read the sentence. *Write it correctly on the lines below, adding or removing apostrophes as needed.*

1. The king ignored the queens demand's.

   _____

   _____

2. "The choice is your's," shed said.

   _____

   _____

3. "Thats great," hed said in reply.

   _____

   _____

4. "Ive gotten all As with you this week anyway."

   _____

   _____

5. "But when mom's aren't happy, nobodys happy."

   _____

   _____

Vocabulary Victory! Do you remember what these words mean? *Check Step 1 if you need a reminder.*

evicted	Apostrophes are going to be rounded up and **evicted** from planet Spelling.
crimson	His neck and face were becoming crimson with anger.
intently	Apostrophes were being **ushered** onto buses.

148

☆ Advanced Guardians Only

Write a paragraph to create sympathy for the apostrophes. *Explain that they are in danger of being recycled. Also explain the confusion that can happen without them, using examples. We will include your paragraph in flyers that will be handed out.* **Hint:** _Indent the first sentence._

_____

_____

_____

_____

_____

_____

_____

_____

_____

_____

_____

_____

_____

_____

_____

_____

_____

_____

_____

_____

Mission 13: Update

Dear guardian friends,

      The apostrophes are back on the job. Thank you! We're (yay for the apostrophe!) so proud of you for helping us return this punctuation mark home. And the sympathetic paragraphs you wrote meant so much to them.

      Keep looking for lost apostrophes. It's possible we missed some. The solutions to this mission are included.

Sincerely,

Kirk, Luke, and Ellen English
Guardians of Grammar Galaxy

Step 1 Solutions

On Guard.

1. A common humor method is:
   surprise   analogy
2. The following is an overused word:
   told   actually
3. What is slang for a shy person?
   wallflower   ride
4. Solve the analogy. **day:night::bees:_____**
   butterflies   fireflies
5. Which prefix means *many*?
   poly-   deca-

Highlight words requiring apostrophes.

1. The kings temper got the best of him because of the crisis.
2. The kids stomachs were rumbling without breakfast.
3. "Its preposterous," the king roared.
4. "Youre going to have more confusion on the planet," he said.
5. "I know well make things right," the queen said.
6. "I havent seen anything like this since the 60s," the king said.
7. "Youll still have to mind your ps and qs," the queen said.
8. "Do you have any 5s I could have as cash?" Luke asked.

Step 2 Solutions – words with removed apostrophes are underlined

1. The queen realized the sweater Ellen was wearing was hers.
2. "It's a sad day when punctuation is detained," the king said.
3. Planet Spelling can't be left to its own any longer.
4. The apostrophes were being transported elsewhere.
5. "Be sure to bring your communicators," the king instructed.
6. "If you don't leave now, you'll risk apostrophes being recycled."
7. "Remember that you're not going to see the A's."
8. "And you shouldn't stop to see any shows."

Step 3 Solutions – words rewritten are underlined

1. The king ignored the queen's demands.
2. "The choice is yours," she'd said.
3. "That's great," he'd said in reply.
4. "I've gotten all A's with you this week anyway."
5. "But when moms aren't happy, nobody's happy."

Mission 14: Hyphens

Dear guardian-friends,

   Have you heard about Better-Together? Father hoped the program would improve-spelling, but instead it has created over-use of hyphens. We need you to use the hyphen-rules we-are sending you and the dictionary to help-us separate hyphens from words where they-don't-belong.

   We hope the hyphenated-words don't give us too-much-trouble about separating.

With-all-our-hearts,

Kirk, Luke, and Ellen English

Guardians of Grammar Galaxy

Hyphens

The word *hyphen* is from the Greek for *together*. Hyphens (-) are used to create some compound words. Note that compound words often begin as separate words. They then become hyphenated and finally become closed compound words with no hyphen. Check a dictionary to determine if a compound word requires a hyphen.

Some examples of hyphenated compound words are check-in, check-up, Commander-in-Chief, President-Elect, mother-in-law, self-esteem, runner-up, singer-songwriter, jack-in-the-box, blue-green, merry-go-round, go-between, pick-me-up, good-for-nothing, two-year-old.

Hyphenate two or more words that describe the following noun. This is called a compound adjective. To determine if it should be hyphenated, ask if each word makes sense describing the noun alone. If not, the words should be hyphenated. Adjective phrases that begin with an -ly adverb and those formed by proper nouns should not be hyphenated.

She was going on a once-in-a-lifetime trip. – *Correct*

The trip was out-of-this-world – Incorrect, adjectives follow the noun

That really-moldy doll should be thrown out. – *Incorrect*

The Red-Star guardian got to work. *Incorrect*

Her easy-come-easy-go approach to life causes problems. – Correct

His my way or the highway attitude causes problems. – *Incorrect; it isn't my attitude or highway attitude, so the words my-way-or-the-highway should be hyphenated.*

Hyphens are also used to continue words that are split at the end of a line. The hyphen must appear between syllables. Check a dictionary if you aren't sure where to hyphenate a word.

Her favorite vocabulary word is *sen-*
sational. – Correct

His friend's family is thinking about ho-
meschooling. – *Incorrect*

⭐ Step 1: On Guard & Remove Unnecessary Hyphens
On Guard. *Highlight the correct answer.*

1. Instead of saying *seriously*:
   use *was like*   leave it out   use *honestly*

2. <u>Don't have a cow!</u> means:
   calm down   don't farm   fantastic

3. Solve the analogy. **king:Gremlin::Little Red Riding Hood:_____?**
   grandmother   wolf   queen

4. Which of the following suffixes means *likely to act?*
   -an   -ance   -ive

5. Use _____ after nouns that possess something.
   hyphens   apostrophes   slang

Say each of these words in a sentence. *Examples are given.*

perspective – viewpoint	I prefer my father's **perspective** that my messy room is no big deal.
admonition – caution	I still hear my mother's **admonition** to look both ways.
superfluous – excessive	I think my sister's use of glitter in her artwork is **superfluous**.

Remove unnecessary hyphens. *Read the sentence. Using correction fluid or a white pen, remove unnecessary hyphens.* **Hint:** <u>*Some sentences will include only necessary hyphens*</u>.

1. The king was furious about the overly-hyphenated newspaper.

2. He wanted to speak to the Editor-in-Chief.

3. He also wanted to talk with what he called his good-for-nothing consultant.

4. But Screen could not locate this snake-in-the-grass.

5. The king was mad at himself for using a consultant as a go-between.

6. But there was no sense throwing a tantrum like a two-year-old.

7. He could depend on his three Grammar-Galaxy guardians.

8. He accepted that his really-brilliant plan had failed.

☆ <u>Step 2: Identify Incorrect Hyphens at the End of Lines</u>
Read the sentence. *Highlight words that are NOT hyphenated correctly between syllables at the end of the line.* **Hint:** <u>Check a dictionary if you aren't sure</u>.

1. Comet, the royal dog, passed his physical with flying color-s, according to his vet.

2. Although Comet is ten years old, the vet feels he will en-joy plenty more years with the family.

3. He has gained a little weight, so table scraps weren't re-commended for him.

4. Because his teeth had some plaque buildup, the doct-or suggested a cleaning.

5. The king said he wasn't sure the cleaning was wor-thy of the extra expense.

6. The queen insisted that Comet have the best ve-terinary care possible.

7. The doctor said Comet's heart was the heart of a five-year-old.

8. The royal children gave Comet a walk in the gard-en after his physical.

Activity. *Count every hyphen you find in a printed article in a magazine or newspaper. Did you find hyphens in a compound word, multi-word adjective, and at the end of lines?*

☆ Step 3: Rewrite Sentences with Correct Hyphenation

Read the sentence. Then write it correctly, including hyphens where they belong.

1. The king was excited about a galaxy wide campaign to improve spelling.

_____

_____

2. The fact that the king was tricked did nothing for his self esteem.

_____

_____

3. The queen was able to reassure him that he was still a good Commander in Chief.

_____

_____

4. It made no sense to play the blame yourself for everything game, she said.

_____

_____

5. She had done that when his mother in law died.

_____

_____

Vocabulary Victory! Do you remember what these words mean? *Check Step 1 if you need a reminder.*

perspective	Sometimes we need a fresh **perspective** on a problem.
admonition	"This is an outrage!" the king continued, ignoring the queen's **admonition**.
superfluous	I better not see this **superfluous** hyphenation in tomorrow's issue.

☆ Advanced Guardians Only

Write why the underlined phrases should NOT be hyphenated. *Refer to the hyphen rules we sent you.* **Hint:** *You may need to check the dictionary*.

1. The king was a <u>positively-grateful</u> man to have the queen for his wife.

   _____

2. She was a woman who was <u>rarer-than-rubies</u>.

   _____

3. She thought he was the best <u>Grammar-Galaxy</u> king ever.

   _____

4. <u>None-the-less</u>, the king had to solve the problem.

   _____

5. Fortunately, the solution seemed to be <u>straight-forward</u>.

   _____

OFFICIAL GUARDIAN MAIL

Mission 14: Update

Dear friends,

     Thanks so much for helping us decide which words to unhyphenate. We aren't sure unhyphenate is a word, but you know what we mean. It turns out the words that didn't need hyphens were relieved when we separated them. Mother always says that too much togetherness isn't a good thing. Now we know why!

     Father said to tell you thanks for helping him solve a problem he started. He is so happy that his *Grammar Gazette* is back to normal. Please keep looking for incorrect hyphens we may have missed. And check the solutions for this mission.

Sincerely,

Kirk, Luke, and Ellen English
Guardians of Grammar Galaxy

<u>Step 1 Solutions</u>

On Guard.

1. Instead of saying *seriously*:
   use *was like*   leave it out   use *honestly*
2. Don't have a cow! means:
   calm down   don't farm   fantastic
3. Solve the analogy. **king:Gremlin::Little Red Riding Hood:____?**
   grandmother   wolf   queen
4. Which of the following suffixes means *likely to act*?
   -an   -ance   -ive
5. Use _____ after nouns that possess something.
   hyphens   apostrophes   slang

Remove unnecessary hyphens. Words with removed hyphens are underlined.

1. The king was furious about the <u>overly hyphenated</u> newspaper.
2. He wanted to speak to the Editor-in-Chief.
3. He also wanted to talk with what he called his good-for-nothing consultant.
4. But Screen could not locate this <u>snake in the grass</u>.
5. The king was mad at himself for using a consultant as a go-between.
6. But there was no sense throwing a tantrum like a two-year-old.
7. He could depend on his three <u>Grammar Galaxy</u> guardians.
8. He accepted that his <u>really brilliant</u> plan had failed.

<u>Step 2 Solutions</u>

1. Comet, the royal dog, passed his physical with flying colors, according to his vet.
2. Although Comet is ten years old, the vet feels he will enjoy plenty more years with the family.
3. He has gained a little weight, so table scraps weren't recommended for him.
4. Because his teeth had some plaque buildup, the doctor suggested a cleaning.
5. The king said he wasn't sure the cleaning was worthy of the extra expense.
6. The queen insisted that Comet have the best veterinary care possible.
7. The doctor said Comet's heart was the heart of a five-year-old.
8. The royal children gave Comet a walk in the garden after his physical

<u>Step 3 Solutions</u> – changes are underlined

1. The king was excited about a <u>galaxy-wide</u> campaign to improve spelling.
2. The fact that the king was tricked did nothing for his <u>self-esteem</u>.
3. The queen was able to reassure him that he was still a good <u>Commander-in-Chief</u>.
4. It made no sense to play the <u>blame-yourself-for-everything</u> game, she said.
5. She had done that when his <u>mother-in-law</u> died..

Advanced Guardians.

1. The king was a <u>positively-grateful</u> man to have the queen for his wife.
   Adjective phrases beginning with -ly adverbs are not hyphenated
2. She was a woman who was <u>rarer-than-rubies</u>.
   Compound adjectives following the noun are not hyphenated.
3. She thought he was the best <u>Grammar-Galaxy</u> king ever.
   Compound adjectives made up of proper nouns are not hyphenated.
4. <u>None-the-less</u>, the king had to solve the problem.
   Nonetheless is a compound word with no hyphens.
5. Fortunately, the solution seemed to be <u>straight-forward</u>.
   Straightforward is a compound adjective that is not hyphenated. The adjective also follows the noun.

162

Mission 15: Tricky Homophones

Dear guardians,

Have you heard about the WOE bill that will require the same spelling of words, regardless of their part of speech? It sounds like spelling would be easier, but unique spellings help us understand what is written.

We have an even better idea than the WOE bill, but we need your help to make it work. With our mother's help, we've created some picture cards that show the differences between homophones. We're calling them Grammar Graphics. If you can show Parliament that these cards improve your spelling, we think we can kill the WOE bill.

Please help us by reviewing the information on tricky homophones. Then complete this mission as soon as possible.

Sincerely,

Kirk, Luke, and Ellen English
Guardians of Grammar Galaxy

Tricky Homophones
Homophones are words that share similar pronunciation but are spelled differently with different meanings. Some of the trickier homophones are related words that require a unique spelling based on their part of speech. For example, *accept* and *except*. *Accept* is a verb meaning consent to receive. I accept your nomination for class president. *Except* is most often a preposition meaning not including. I will buy everything you have except for the orange socks. **A list of a few other tricky homophones, their meanings, and parts of speech follows.**

advice	information	noun
advise	give counsel	verb
affect	make a difference / emotion	verb / noun
effect	change / cause	noun / verb
ate	consumed	verb
eight	number	adjective
bare	empty	adjective
bear	large mammal	noun
blue	color	adjective
blew	gusted	verb
bored	uninterested / form a hole	adjective / verb
board	piece of wood	noun
brake	device to slow or stop / slow or stop	noun / verb
break	shatter or destroy	verb
buy	purchase / a purchase	verb / noun
by	indicating / go past	preposition / adverb
counsel	guide / advice; lawyers	verb / noun
council	group of advisors	noun
do	perform	verb / helping verb
dew	tiny drops of water	noun
here	at this place	adverb
hear	perceive with the ear	verb
know	be aware; familiar with	verb
no	zero / not at all	adjective / adverb

lose	no longer have; unable to find	verb
loose	not firm or tight / set free	adjective / verb
made	formed	verb
maid	housecleaner	noun
our	belonging to us	possessive pronoun
hour	sixty minutes	noun
passed	leave behind	verb
past	time before	noun / adjective
peak	top	noun
peek	look quickly	verb
plain	undecorated; easy	adjective
plane	aircraft; flat surface	noun
their	belonging to them	possessive pronoun
there	at a place	adverb
they're	they are	contraction
then	at that time; therefore	adverb
than	used in comparisons	conjunction / preposition
threw	sent with force	verb
through	moving through something / toward completion	preposition / adverb
to	identifying location or noun	preposition
two	number	adjective
too	also; excessive	adverb
weather	state of atmosphere / wear away	noun / verb
whether	expressing doubt or alternatives	conjunction
your	belonging to 'you'	possessive pronoun
you're	you are	contraction

⭐ Step 1: On Guard & Choose the Right Homophone

On Guard. *Use a highlighter to mark TRUE or FALSE for each question.*

1. President-Elect should be hyphenated.   TRUE   FALSE

2. The possessive pronoun her's should always have an apostrophe.   TRUE   FALSE

3. The prefix sub- means under or below.   TRUE   FALSE

4. To solve an analogy, determine the relationship between the first word pair.   TRUE   FALSE

5. My old lady is foxy. means my grandma is clever.   TRUE   FALSE

Say each of these words in a sentence. *Examples are given.*

assent – agreement	I did not give my brother my **assent** to take my pillow.
apprised – informed	My friend kept me **apprised** of what went on while I was sick.
replete – full	My drawer is **replete** with candy wrappers, rocks, and coins.

Choose the right homophone. *Read the sentence. Highlight the homophone that belongs in the blank using the part of speech in parentheses as a clue. Use the list of tricky homophones we sent you for help.*

1. **The king has relied on the Prime Minister's _____ before. (noun)**

    advice   advise

2. **If the WOE bill passes _____ Parliament, the galaxy is in trouble. (preposition)**

    threw   through

3. **The king didn't care _____ the polls supported the bill. (conjunction)**

    weather   whether

4. **The king realized most people didn't _____ what the bill was about. (verb)**

    know   no

5. **"_____ planet depends on unique spellings," the king said. (possessive pronoun)**

    Our   Hour

6. **"We will have to decide our next move _____." (adverb)**

    then   than

7. **"_____ going to have to ask the guardians for help." (contraction)**

    You're   Your

8. **"Just tell us what to _____ first," Kirk said. (verb)**

    do   dew

167

☆ Step 2: Use Grammar Graphics to Choose the Right Homophone

Study the Grammar Graphics. *Then read the sentences. Highlight the homophone that belongs in the blank.*

1. **Luke said he was as hungry as a _____.**
   bare   bear
2. **He also said he was _____ while lying on a wood deck.**
   bored   board
3. **The king is always willing to _____ for birds.**
   brake   break
4. **The king says he is happy he doesn't live _____ a store.**
   by   buy
5. **Kirk enjoys hammering nails into a _____.**
   bored   board
6. **When Ellen bakes, she likes to _____ the eggs.**
   brake   break
7. **The queen prefers to _____ ; the king prefers to borrow.**
   by   buy
8. **Cook isn't happy when her cupboards are _____.**
   bare   bear

168

Activity. Homophones are frequently misused in casual writing. Ask your teacher to show you social media posts that contain these mistakes. See if you can identify them. You may also check GrammarGalaxyBooks.com/RedStar for examples.

⭐ Step 3: Write the Homophone That Belongs in the Sentence
Study the Grammar Graphics. Then write the correct homophone in the blank.

1. Luke doesn't like to _____ spaceball games.

2. The queen complains that the king often doesn't _____ her.

3. Ellen was excited when her car _____ Luke's on the track.

4. In an argument, the queen says not to bring up the _____.

5. Luke _____ a ball that hit a castle window.

6. "Come _____ immediately," the queen had said.

7. "We've gone _____ the rules about spaceball before."

8. "You'll stay in your room until I turn you _____."

Vocabulary Victory! Do you remember what these words mean? *Check Step 1 if you need a reminder.*

assent	"I won't give my **assent**," the king said.
apprised	The Prime Minister promised to keep the king **apprised** of the bill's progress.
replete	The Internet was **replete** with ads discussing the unfairness words faced with spelling.

☆ Advanced Guardians Only

Create your own Grammar Graphics to remember tricky homophones. *Consider making cards for ate/eight, blue/blew, our/hour, made/maid, peak/peek, plain/plane, or weather/whether. Draw pictures or print pictures you find online. Be sure to write the correct homophone under each picture.*

Mission 15: Update

Dear guardian friends,

   We are so excited! The WOE bill is dead. Tricky homophones are one of the big reasons we make spelling mistakes. You've proven to Parliament that Grammar Graphics help you remember the difference between homophones. Spelling has improved and the WOE bill isn't needed.

   We all like it when our names are spelled correctly, right? We feel important. The homophones feel the same way. Now that we've been spelling them correctly, they're happier. They don't want to be spelled the same way as other homophones.

   Thank you for keeping the galaxy strong! We are including the solutions to this mission.

Sincerely,

Kirk, Luke, and Ellen English
Guardians of Grammar Galaxy

Step 1 Solutions

On Guard.

1.	President-Elect should be hyphenated.	TRUE FALSE
2.	The possessive pronoun her's should always have an apostrophe.	TRUE FALSE
3.	The prefix sub- means under or below.	TRUE FALSE
4.	To solve an analogy, determine the relationship between the first word pair.	TRUE FALSE
5.	My old lady is foxy. means my grandma is clever.	TRUE FALSE

Choose the right homophone.

1. The king has relied on the Prime Minister's _____ before. (noun)
advice   advise

2. If the WOE bill passes _____ Parliament, the galaxy is in trouble. (preposition)
threw   through

3. The king didn't care _____ the polls supported the bill. (conjunction)
weather   whether

4. The king realized most people didn't _____ what the bill was about. (verb)
know   no

5. "_____ planet depends on unique spellings," the king said. (possessive pronoun)
Our   Hour

6. "We will have to decide our next move _____." (adverb)
then   than

7. "_____ going to have to ask the guardians for help." (contraction)
You're   You

8. "Just tell us what to _____ first," Kirk said. (verb)
do   dew

Step 2 Solutions

1. Luke said he was as hungry as a _____.
bare   bear

2. He also said he was _____ while lying on a wood deck.
bored   board

3. The king is always willing to _____ for birds.
brake   break

4. The king says he is happy he doesn't live _____ a store.
by   buy

5. Kirk enjoys hammering nails into a _____.
bored   board

6. When Ellen bakes, she likes to _____ the eggs.
brake   break

7. The queen prefers to _____ ; the king prefers to borrow.
by   buy

8. Cook isn't happy when her cupboards are _____.
bare   bear

Step 3 Solutions

1. Luke doesn't like to lose spaceball games.
2. The queen complains that the king often doesn't hear her.
3. Ellen was excited when her car passed Luke's on the track.
4. In an argument, the queen says not to bring up the past.
5. Luke threw a ball that hit a castle window.
6. "Come here immediately," the queen had said.
7. "We've gone through the rules about spaceball before."
8. "You'll stay in your room until I turn you loose."

Mission 16: Shades of Meaning

Dear mind-blowing guardians,

We are having a problem with the specific meanings of vocabulary words, and we know why. Words have been moved to random floors of their buildings because of the Fairness Act, regardless of their shade of meaning. Father has called on the Supreme Court to decide that the Fairness Act doesn't apply to vocabulary words. Until there's a ruling on that, we want to put these words back where they belong. The trouble is, we don't know which words are more intense than others.

Using the information below, please complete this mission and help us with this catastrophe-- or problem. We aren't sure which it is.

Earnestly,

Kirk, Luke, and Ellen English
Guardians of Grammar Galaxy

Shades of Meaning
Words can be synonyms (similar) yet still be different in intensity. For example, *good* and *spectacular* are synonyms, but the word *spectacular* has a higher intensity than good. *Mad* and *furious* are synonyms with *furious* having a higher intensity than mad. To communicate well, it is important to choose the synonym with the correct shade of meaning. Rather than choosing any synonym from a thesaurus, read definitions and example sentences. Make sure the synonym and your intended meaning match.

⭐ Step 1: On Guard & Identify the Word of Intensity

On Guard. *Highlight the correct answer for each statement.*

1. <u>Accept</u> is a:
      verb   preposition

2. Two or more words that form an adjective describing a following noun should be:
      capitalized   hyphenated

3. Apostrophes are used in:
      contractions   possessive pronouns that end in s

4. The prefix that means *opposite* is:
      anti-   fore-

5. Word analogies are a test of:
      personality   vocabulary

Say each of these words in a sentence. *Examples are given.*

beseechingly – pleadingly	I didn't give up my favorite sweater, even though my sister asked **beseechingly**.
torn– undecided	I'm **torn** about choosing the chocolate or vanilla.
mobility – movement	My leg fell asleep, affecting my **mobility**.

Identify the word of intensity. *Read the sentence. Highlight the word with the <u>greater</u> intensity that belongs in the blank. You may need to use a dictionary to determine the words' intensity.*

1. Ernie was _____ about the long wait in line.
      bothered   exasperated

2. The king was _____ that Ernie hadn't brought his wallet.
      irritated   rankled

3. Ernie was _____ that they got a ride to the front.
      thrilled   happy

4. The king was _____ about the news coverage.
      unsettled   agitated

5. The queen was _____ about the king's behavior.
      distressed   concerned

6. The king was _____ after a long day.
      exhausted   tired

7. The children were in _____ of the planet's status.
      doubt   disbelief

8. The king was _____ his children's plan.
      pleased with   proud of

177

⭐ Step 2: Choose Low- and High-Intensity Synonyms

Use the word box to complete the chart of low and high intensity synonyms for each word. *Write the words in the correct column. You may need to use a dictionary to determine the words' intensity.*

little	humongous	miniscule
warm	light	chilly
dim	leisurely	sharp
luminous	murky	large
sluggish	scorching	frigid
genius	arduous	accessible

Word	Low-Intensity Synonym	High-Intensity Synonym
big		
small		
hot		
cold		
bright		
dark		
slow		
smart		

Activity. *Communicate with your family today using the wrong shade of meaning for your vocabulary words. For example, you might say that you are livid when you're just a little upset. If they notice, explain that you are learning about shades of meaning.*

⭐ Step 3: Write a Low-Intensity Synonym

For each underlined word, write a low-intensity synonym. *Use a thesaurus or dictionary as needed.*

1. The king <u>adores</u> the game of golf.

_____

2. Ernie was <u>impatient</u> to leave for the tournament.

_____

3. The king <u>savored</u> the food he had.

_____

4. Ernie's shirt purchase was <u>extravagant</u>.

_____

5. The reporter's questions were <u>multitudinous</u>.

_____

Vocabulary Victory! Do you remember what these words mean? *Check Step 1 if you need a reminder.*

beseechingly	"Okay, how about the space porter then" Ernie asked **beseechingly**.
torn	The king was obviously **torn** as he estimated their wait time.
mobility	A tournament staff member drove a few attendees with **mobility** challenges in a golf cart.

⭐ <u>Advanced Guardians Only</u>

Write your testimony for the Supreme Court about why the Fairness Act is a bad idea. *Use a personal example of how using the wrong shade of meaning could cause problems for you on your birthday. Be sure to sign your name in cursive and date your testimony.*

_____

_____

_____

_____

_____

_____

_____

_____

_____

_____

_____

_____

_____

_____

_____

_____

_____

_____

Signed,   Date

_____   _____

Mission 16: Update

Dear faithful guardians,

    Your help in assigning words their shade of meaning was invaluable, and we do mean invaluable! We were able to put the words back on the floors where they were living. The even better news is that after reviewing your testimony, the Supreme Court ruled the Fairness Act doesn't apply to words.

    Just in case we were wrong about any word's shade of meaning, please check the solutions to this mission.

Sincerely,

Kirk, Luke, and Ellen English
Guardians of Grammar Galaxy

Step 1 Solutions

On Guard.

1. <u>Accept</u> is a:
   verb   preposition
2. Two or more words that form <u>an adjective describing a following noun</u> should be:
   capitalized   hyphenated
3. Apostrophes are used in:
   contractions   possessive pronouns that end in s
4. The prefix that means *opposite* is:
   anti-   fore-
5. Word analogies are a test of:
   personality   vocabulary

Identify the word of intensity.

1. Ernie was _____ about the long wait in line.
   bothered   exasperated
2. The king was _____ that Ernie hadn't brought his wallet.
   irritated   rankled
3. Ernie was _____ that they got a ride to the front.
   thrilled   happy
4. The king was _____ about the news coverage.
   unsettled   agitated
5. The queen was _____ about the king's behavior.
   distressed   concerned
6. The king was _____ after a long day.
   exhausted   tired
7. The children were in _____ of the planet's status.
   doubt   disbelief
8. The king was _____ his children's plan.
   pleased with   proud of

Step 2 Solutions

Word	Low-Intensity Synonym	High-Intensity Synonym
big	large	humongous
small	little	miniscule
hot	warm	scorching
cold	chilly	frigid
bright	light	luminous
dark	dim	murky
slow	leisurely	sluggish
smart	sharp	genius

Step 3 Solutions – answers may vary

1. The king <u>adores</u> the game of golf.
   likes

2. Ernie was <u>impatient</u> to leave for the tournament.
   eager

3. The king <u>savored</u> the food he had.
   enjoyed

4. Ernie's shirt purchase was <u>extravagant</u>.
   expensive

5. The reporter's questions were <u>multitudinous</u>.
   many

182

Mission 17: Writing with Numbers

Dear friends and fellow guardians,

We don't know if you've heard the news or not, but an unauthorized ship filled with numerals landed on planet Spelling. At first it didn't seem like numerals could live there, but we have learned we can use them in our writing. Your mission is to find a job for the numbers on planet Spelling. Please use the guidelines from *The Guide to Grammar Galaxy on the next page to help you complete the mission.*

Gratefully,

Kirk, Luke, and Luke English

Guardians of Grammar Galaxy

Writing with Numbers

Numbers should sometimes be spelled out and at other times should be left as numerals in writing.

WHEN TO SPELL OUT NUMBERS

- **Numbers one to nine should be spelled out.** The girl grabbed *five* pencils.

- **Numbers at the beginning of a sentence should be spelled out or the sentence rearranged.** *Sixteen* students enrolled in the class. The school enrolled *16* students.

- **When numbers appear next to each other in the text, one number should be spelled out.** He ordered *75 nine*-inch nails.

- **In dialogue or quotes, numbers should generally be spelled out.** "I'm going to need *fifty* cupcakes."

- **When spelling out numbers, two-word numbers under 100 should be hyphenated.** "I counted out one hundred twenty-five buttons."

WHEN TO USE NUMERALS

- **Use numerals for dates and numbers larger than nine.** By *1865*, more than *600,000* soldiers had died in the Civil War.

- **Use numerals for decimals. (Add a zero for decimals less than one.)** The chance of being struck by lightning in your lifetime is *0.0003* or 1 in 3000.

- **Use numerals to stay consistent in describing something in a sentence, even if it breaks another rule.** She counted *5* of *20* pens that worked.

- **Use numerals in science writing or directions.** Add *4* ounces of vinegar to *2 ½* tablespoons of baking soda.

WHEN TO USE BOTH SPELLING AND NUMERALS

- **When writing about millions and billions, mix numerals and words.** Over *140 million* books have been published to date.

- **When choosing whether to spell a number or use a numeral in writing, use a style guide.** Or ask the teacher or publication you're writing for.

⭐ Step 1: On Guard & Highlight the Correct Numerical Format

On Guard. *Answer the questions or answer them verbally for your teacher.*

1. What is a shade of meaning in vocabulary?

2. What is a homophone?

3. How can you know for sure when a word should be hyphenated?

4. What punctuation mark is used to show possession?

5. What is the difference between a prefix and a suffix?

Say each of these words in a sentence. *Examples are given.*

Inopportune – inconvenient	I told my mom that it was an **inopportune** time to do chores.
impending – coming	Mom reminded me of Grandma's **impending** visit.
expedition – trip	I'm looking forward to our **expedition** to the wild animal park.

Highlight the correct numerical format. *Read the sentence. Then highlight the numbers that are correctly formatted for the blank.*

1. **The lowest golf score on an 18-hole course is** _____.
   fifty-five   55

2. **The golf course record was set in** _____.
   two thousand 12   2012

3. **Beginning golfers should start on a course with** _____ **holes.**
   nine   9

4. **The secret to Cook's cookies is** _____ **tablespoons of cream cheese.**
   two   2

5. **Cook bakes her cookies at** _____ **degrees Celsius.**
   one hundred sixty-three   163

6. **Cook is reading a book called** *The* _____ *Plan.*
   Ten Million   *10 Million*

7. **Cook says the odds of winning the lottery are** _____.
   .000000014   0.000000014

8. **Only** _____ **of the 24 cookies she baked are left.**
   six   6

☆ Step 2: Find Incorrectly Written Numbers

Highlight numbers written incorrectly in each sentence.
Use the guidebook information we sent you for help. **Hint:**
Some sentences may not have incorrect numbers.

1. Cook has been investing for fifteen years.

2. 40 years ago, Cook's parents began saving their money.

3. Her father always said, "Ten dollars saved today can be a million dollars tomorrow."

4. He also taught her about the stock market crash of 1929.

5. She tried to save four of every 10 dollars she made.

6. Her savings account only pays .1 percent interest.

7. That's why she invests in thirty different stocks that pay dividends.

8. She hopes to have more than five million dollars saved when she retires.

Activity. Play a board game that uses two dice. Every time someone says the number rolled that is nine or under, it must be spelled out. Otherwise, the turn is lost.

★ Step 3: Write the Correct Number

Using a number from the box, write a correctly formatted number in the blank that makes sense. *Use the guidebook information to help you.*

10	three hundred twenty-five	8
325	Ten	millionaire
eighteen	one	thirty-six
1,000,00-aire	18	1
forty-eight	36	1929

1. Cook has been working since she was _____.

2. _____ years ago, she started working for the royal family.

3. She is saving to be a _____.

3. Her cookie recipe calls for _____ teaspoon of baking soda.

4. She bakes her cookies at _____ degrees Fahrenheit.

5. She bakes 3 dozen at once, which is _____.

Vocabulary Victory! Do you remember what these words mean? *Check Step 1 if you need a reminder.*

assent	"I won't give my **assent**," the king said.
apprised	The Prime Minister promised to keep the king **apprised** of the bill's progress.
replete	The Internet was **replete** with ads discussing the unfairness words faced with spelling.

☆ <u>Advanced Guardians Only</u>

Complete Wacky Words with numbers. *Write the numbers and other information requested in the blanks below. Then write the information into the lettered blanks on the next page and read what you've written. Don't peek and you'll have written something funny.* **Hint:** <u>*Numeral means a number you don't spell*</u>.

a. _____ numeral under 100

b. _____ four-digit year

c. _____ kitchen appliance

d. _____ famous person

e. _____ food

f. _____ numeral over 300

g. _____ any numeral

h. _____ place in home

Best Chocolate Chip Cookie Recipe

by _____ (d)

Created in _____ (b)

Serves _____ (g)

Preheat the oven to _____ (f) degrees

In a medium bowl, combine _____ (a) cups flour, 1 tsp. baking soda, baking powder, and sea salt.

Using a _____(c) combine _____ T. butter (a), and _____ cups (g) brown sugar until light and creamy, about _____ (a) minutes.

Add in _____ (e) and _____ (a)large eggs. Gradually beat in flour mixture and stir in chocolate chips.

Wrap dough in plastic and store in _____ (h) for (g) _____ hours.

Drop dough by _____(g)-tablespoon sized balls onto baking sheets. Bake for _____ (a) minutes.

Mission 17: Update

Dear guardians,

　　The numbers on planet Spelling love the work you've given them to do. They say they would like to stay here. We appreciate them and want them to stay too. What the Gremlin meant for evil, we used for good! That's especially true with Cook's Out-of-This-World Chocolate Chip Cookies.

　　We are sending you the mission solutions to check. We want the numerals to have the best jobs for them here in the galaxy.

Serving with you 24/7,

Kirk, Luke, and Ellen English

Guardians of Grammar Galaxy

P.S. You've completed the Spelling & Vocabulary Unit. Please review what you've learned. Then take the Spelling & Vocabulary Challenge. Do your best to get at last nine correct.

Step 1 Solutions

On Guard.

1. **What is a shade of meaning in vocabulary?** Synonyms that differ in intensity.

2. **What is a homophone?** Homophones are words that share similar pronunciation but are spelled differently with different meanings.

3. **How can you know for sure when a word should be hyphenated?** Check a dictionary.

4. **What punctuation mark is used to show possession?** apostrophe

5. **What is the difference between a prefix and a suffix?** A prefix is at the beginning of a root word; a suffix is at the end of a root word.

Highlight the correct numerical format.

1. **The lowest golf score on an 18-hole course is _____.**
   fifty-five   55
2. **The golf course record was set in _____.**
   two thousand 12   2012
3. **Beginning golfers should start on a course with _____ holes.**
   nine   9
4. **The secret to Cook's cookies is _____ tablespoons of cream cheese.**
   two   2
5. **Cook bakes her cookies at _____ degrees Celsius.**
   one hundred sixty-three   163
6. **Cook is reading a book called** *The* _____ *Plan.*
   Ten Million   10 Million
7. **Cook says the odds of winning the lottery are _____.**
   .000000014   0.000000014
8. **Only _____ of the 24 cookies she baked are left.**
   six   6

Step 2 Solutions

1. Cook has been investing for fifteen years.
2. 40 years ago, Cook's parents began saving their money.
3. Her father always said, "Ten dollars saved today can be a million dollars tomorrow."
4. He also taught her about the stock market crash of 1929.
5. She tried to save four of every 10 dollars she made.
6. Her savings account only pays .1 percent interest.
7. That's why she invests in thirty different stocks that pay dividends.
8. She hopes to have more than five million dollars saved when she retires.

Step 3 Solutions

1. Cook has been working since she was 18.
2. Ten years ago, she started working for the royal family.
3. She is saving to be a millionaire.
4. 3. Her cookie recipe calls for 1 teaspoon of baking soda.
5. She bakes her cookies at 325 degrees Fahrenheit.
6. She bakes 3 dozen at once, which is 36.

Spelling & Vocabulary Challenge I

Carefully read all the possible answers and then highlight the letter for the __one__ best answer.

1. **Numbers one to nine should be:**
   a. spelled out
   b. written as numerals
   c. sent back to Math Galaxy

2. **__Furious__ has a higher _____ than __mad__:**
   a. intensity
   b. IQ
   c. analogy

3. **Which word belongs in the blank? I need your _____.**
   a. advise
   b. advice
   c. council

4. **What belongs in the blank? I gave the baby a _____.**
   a. really-cute doll
   b. jack in the box
   c. jack-in-the-box

5. **What belongs in the blank? I gave the dog _____ bone.**
   a. it's
   b. its
   c. a cows'

6. **What word or prefix belongs in the blank? The police said the crime wasn't committed in their _____diction.**
   a. anti
   b. sub
   c. juris

7. Solve the analogy. deca-:centi::centi:_____
   a. multi-
   b. mille-
   c. poly-

8. Solve the analogy. act:active::sense::_____
   a. sensitive
   b. sensory
   c. sensation

9. <u>Frenemy</u> is:
   a. a homophone
   b. a root word
   c. Portmanteau slang

10. Rewrite the sentence: Audrey was like "I'm not going."
   a. Audrey said, "I'm not going."
   b. Audrey literally said, "I'm not going."
   c. neither a nor b

Number Correct:_____/10

⭐ *Advanced Guardian Vocabulary Challenge*
For an extra challenge, highlight the word that belongs in each blank.

1. **My friend approached my pet snake with _____.**
   fuming   beverages   trepidation

2. **I'm in trouble because I broke an _____ vase.**
   ornate   relay   adjoining

3. **Our mother tells us it's rude to make _____ comments.**
   lad   snide   adored

4. **She _____ about what she would eat if she owned a candy store.**
   mused   ushered   intently

5. **I _____ my sister from my room, even though it's her room too.**
   crimson   evicted   splurge

6. **I think my sister's use of glitter in her artwork is _____.**
   admonition   torn   superfluous

7. **I did not give my brother my _____ to take my pillow.**
   assent   apprised   replete

8. **My leg fell asleep, affecting my _____.**
   perspective   mobility   beseechingly

9. **I'm looking forward to our _____ to the wild animal park.**
   expedition   impending   inopportune

Number Correct:_____/9

Spelling & Vocabulary Challenge 1 Answers
1.a; 2.a; 3.b; 4.c; 5.b; 6.c; 7.b; 8.a; 9.c; 10.a

If you got 9 or more correct, congratulations! You've earned your Spelling & Vocabulary star. You may add it to your Grammar Guardian bookmark. You are ready for an adventure in grammar.

If you did not get 9 or more correct, don't worry. You have another chance. You may want to review the information in the guidebook for each story you've read so far. Then take the Spelling & Vocabulary Challenge 2. Remember to **choose the one best answer**.

Advanced Guardian Vocabulary Challenge Answers
1. trepidation
2. ornate
3. snide
4. mused
5. evicted
6. superfluous
7. assent
8. mobility
9. expedition

Spelling & Vocabulary Challenge 2

Carefully read all the possible answers and then highlight the letter for the **one** best answer.

1. **Which is the correct way to write the plural of the letter i?**
   a. i's
   b. is
   c. eyes

2. **You should use numerals in:**
   a. science writing
   b. directions
   c. both a and b

3. **The word buy means:**
   a. purchase
   b. next to
   c. farewell

4. **What belongs in the blank? He took his _____ son to the zoo.**
   a. 2 year old
   b. 2-year-old
   c. two-year-old

5. **What belongs in the blank? _____ not a good day for swimming.**
   a. Its
   b. It's
   c. Isn't

6. **What belongs in the blank? My two _____ friends are over playing.**
   a. girls'
   b. girl's
   c. girls's

7. **Solve the analogy. milli:kilo::multi:_____**
   a. deca
   b. semi
   c. poly

8. **Solve the analogy. ject:throw::sub:**
   a. anti
   b. under
   c. before

9. **Jargon is a form of:**
   a. slang
   b. apostrophe
   c. both a and b

10. **Rewrite this sentence without overused words or slang. <u>Olivia is a nice girl.</u>**
   a. Olivia is a totally nice girl.
   b. Olivia is a foxy girl.
   c. Olivia is a polite girl.

Number Correct:_____/10

Spelling & Vocabulary Challenge 2 Answers
1.a; 2.c; 3.a; 4.c; 5.b; 6.a; 7.c; 8.b; 9.a; 10.c

If you got 9 or more correct, congratulations! You've earned your Spelling & Vocabulary star. You may add a star to your bookmark. You are now ready for an adventure in grammar.

If you did not get 9 or more correct, don't worry. Review the questions you missed with your teacher. You may want to get more practice using the resources at GrammarGalaxyBooks.com/RedStar. Your teacher can ask you other questions like the ones you missed and if you get them correct, you'll have earned your Spelling & Vocabulary star and can move on to an adventure in grammar.

Unit III: Adventures in Grammar

Mission 18: Participles

Dear guardians,

     We'd be ly—; we wouldn't be tell—. We are disappointed that we have to interrupt the Galaxy Cup with a mission. But it's necessary.

     Participles on planet Sentence are tailgat—. They are at a party and can't be used. We have an idea to get them participat— again. Please complete this mission while we go to planet Sentence. We hope to get you back to watch— the match ASAP. We are including information on participles to help you.

Sincerely,

Kirk, Luke, and Ellen English
Guardians of Grammar Galaxy

Participles

Participles are verb forms that can be used as part of a multi-word verb, as adjectives, or as nouns. Participles are present or past in form. Participles used as adjectives or nouns are also known as verbals.

Participles as Verbs (Actions)

Present participles always end in -*ing*.

I have been *listening* to the music for hours.

have – helping verb; been – past participle; listening – present participle

Past participles for regular verbs end in -ed.

I had *listened* to the music for hours.

had – helping verb; listened – past participle

Past participles for irregular verbs vary.

I have *bought* you some new music.

have – helping verb; bought – past participle, irregular verb

Participles as Adjectives (Descriptors)

Participles as adjectives may be present or past.

I have a new *swimming* suit. – present

I ran into the *closed* door. – past

Participles as Nouns/Gerunds (Things)

Gerunds always end in -ing.

Swimming is my favorite sport.

I don't like *lying*.

⭐ Step 1: On Guard & Find the Participles

On Guard. *Read the sentence. Highlight the best answer.*

1. _____ eggs make a dozen.
   12   Twelve   2 sets of 6

2. His heart was pounding, and his eyes darted wildly because he was _____.
   afraid   scared   terrified

3. The kids were excited to get on the _____ and start their trip.
   plane   plain   playne

4. She paid a lot for the _____ painting.
   one of a kind   one-of-a-kind   one of-a-kind

5. My grandfather was a kid in the _____.
   '50s   1950's   nineteen fifties

Say each of these words in a sentence. *Examples are given.*

tersely – shortly	The rude cashier answered me **tersely**.
contained – controlled	The babysitter worked hard to keep the toddlers **contained**.
aerial – midair	I have an **aerial** view of my room from the top bunk.

Find the participles. *Read the sentence. Highlight the participle, using the type of participle given in parentheses as a clue.*

1. The king had just finished his workout. (verb)

2. The exhausted king took a nap. (adjective)

3. Tailgating is a party outside a stadium. (noun/gerund)

4. Excited words gathered on planet Sentence. (adjective)

5. One of the king's favorite activities is eating. (noun/gerund)

6. A thundering cheer rose from the stadium. (adjective)

7. People had been waiting for the game for months. (verb)

8. Players wore jogging suits to the field. (adjective)

⭐ Step 2: Identify the Type of Participle

Highlight the part of speech of the participle underlined in each sentence. *Use the information we sent you on participles if you need it.*

1. The <u>cheering</u> fans greeted the players.
    verb   adjective   noun

2. Many players had been <u>waiting</u> for the match all their lives.
    verb   adjective   noun

3. <u>Halting</u> speech affected the announcers.
    verb   adjective   noun

4. Cook had made burgers in a <u>frying</u> pan.
    verb   adjective   noun

5. The king loved the burgers' crisp, <u>fried</u> edges.
    verb   adjective   noun

6. <u>Waiting</u> wasn't something Luke did patiently.
    verb   adjective   noun

7. Luke had not heard of <u>tailgating</u> before.
    verb   adjective   noun

8. The game had <u>begun</u> when they realized what was wrong.
    verb   adjective   noun

Activity. For your teacher, *say a sentence with a participle as a verb, then a sentence with a participle as an adjective, and finally a sentence with a gerund that all make sense together. Bonus points if you use humor.*

☆ Step 3: Write a Participle

Write a participle in the blank that makes sense. *Use a form of the verb in parentheses.*

1. Most of the men had been _____ soccer all their lives. (play)

2. A well _____ goal is a goalie's focus. (defend)

3. The _____ player hung his head in shame. (penalize)

4. _____ is one of the first skills players develop. (dribble)

5. _____ the ball is only allowed by goalies. (punt)

6. _____ means to take the ball away from the opponent with the feet. (tackle)

7. Fans have been _____ for hours. (wait)

8. A _____ player must have his foot planted firmly. (shoot)

Vocabulary Victory! Do you remember what these words mean? *Check Step 1 if you need a reminder.*

tersely	"Yes," he said **tersely**.
contained	I've called in extra Grammar Patrol to keep it **contained**.
aerial	Screen immediately responded with an **aerial** view of a large gathering of words.

☆ <u>Advanced Guardians Only</u>
Write rules for a game you like, including many participles. *We hope to get participles playing games so we can use them again.*
Hint: *Use -ed and -ing verbs as adjectives or nouns.*

1. _____

2. _____

3. _____

4. _____

5. _____

6. _____

7. _____

8. _____

Mission 18: Update

Dear guardians,

     It worked! The participles had so much fun playing together in sentences. As soon as they started, the Galaxy Cup went smoothly. We have another completed mission. Completed is a participle. Did you catch that? Guarding is another participle and we're so glad to be guarding participles with you.

     When you're through watching the game, be sure to make sure your mission was completed correctly. The solutions follow.

Sincerely,

Kirk, Luke, and Ellen English
Guardians of Grammar Galaxy

Step 1 Solutions

On Guard.

1. _____ eggs make a dozen.
   12   Twelve   2 sets of 6

2. His heart was pounding, and his eyes darted wildly because he was _____.
   afraid   scared   terrified

3. The kids were excited to get on the _____ and start their trip.
   plane   plain   playne

4. She paid a lot for the _____ painting.
   one of a kind   one-of-a-kind   one of-a-kind

5. My grandfather was a kid in the _____.
   '50s   1950's   nineteen fifties

Find the participles.

1. The king had just finished his workout. (verb)
2. The exhausted king took a nap. (adjective)
3. Tailgating is a party outside a stadium. (noun/gerund)
4. Excited words gathered on planet Sentence. (adjective)
5. One of the king's favorite activities is eating. (noun/gerund)
6. A thundering cheer rose from the stadium. (adjective)
7. People had been waiting for the game for months. (verb)
8. Players wore jogging suits to the field. (adjective)

Step 2 Solutions

1. The cheering fans greeted the players.
   verb   adjective   noun
2. Many players had been waiting for the match all their lives.
   verb   adjective   noun
3. Halting speech affected the announcers.
   verb   adjective   noun
4. Cook had made burgers in a frying pan.
   verb   adjective   noun
5. The king loved the burgers' crisp, fried edges.
   verb   adjective   noun
6. Waiting wasn't something Luke did patiently.
   verb   adjective   noun
7. Luke had not heard of tailgating before.
   verb   adjective   noun
8. The game had begun when they realized what was wrong.
   verb   adjective   noun

Step 3 Solutions

1. Most of the men had been playing soccer all their lives. (play)

2. A well defended goal is a goalie's focus. (defend)

3. The penalized player hung his head in shame. (penalize)

4. Dribbling is one of the first skills players develop. (dribble)

5. Punting the ball is only allowed by goalies. (punt)

6. Tackling means to take the ball away from the opponent with the feet. (tackle)

7. Fans have been waiting for hours. (wait)

8. A shooting player must have his foot planted firmly. (shoot)

Mission 19: Objects of Prepositions

Dear guardian friends,

Those of you who are participating in the Grammar Dash may not be surprised to get this mission. The race director couldn't describe the obstacles to us because objects of prepositions are missing.

We are on our way to planet Sentence to find them, but we need your help. Find objects of prepositions quickly enough, and we may be able to run the race as planned. We are including the information you need. Father is giving a long speech on the importance of good grammar to delay the start.

Sincerely,

Kirk, Luke, and Ellen English

Guardians of Grammar Galaxy

Objects of Prepositions
The noun or pronoun at the end of a prepositional phrase is the object of the preposition. The object of the preposition answers the question *What?* after the preposition.   **He is afraid of the dark.**   *Of* is the preposition. *Afraid of what?* Dark. *Dark* is the object of the preposition (OP). Modifiers or descriptors of the object of the preposition are separate parts of speech.   **I love to sleep in a big, comfy bed.**   *In* is the preposition. *Sleep in what?* Bed. *Bed* is the OP. The word *a* is an article adjective, while *big* and *comfy* are adjectives describing *bed*.

☆ Step 1: On Guard & Review Prepositions

On Guard. *Highlight the correct answer for the following sentence:*
The size seven shoes Ellen found lying in the closet were her's.

1. Which of these is the present participle in the sentence?
   found   lying   shoes

2. Which of these words in the sentence should be hyphenated?
   size-seven   found-lying   in-the-closet

3. What is the object of the preposition in the sentence?
   hers   shoes   closet

4. How should the possessive word in the sentence be written?
   her's   hers   her

5. How should the number in the sentence be written?
   seven   7   11

Say each of these words in a sentence. *Examples are given.*

morose – down	I was pretty **morose** about not getting a pet snake for my birthday.
reverie – daydream	My brother has been in a **reverie** ever since the new space movie came out.
encounter – meet	My dream is to have a dolphin **encounter** and swim with one.

212

Review prepositions. *Sing the prepositions song to the tune of Yankee Doodle. Find a link to listen at GrammarGalaxyBooks.com/RedStar. Then highlight the prepositions in the sentences that follow.* **Hint:** <u>*There may be more than one preposition in each sentence*</u>.

VERSE 1:
Aboard, about, above, across
Against, along, around
Amid, among, after, at
Except, for, during, down

VERSE 2:
Behind, below, beneath, beside
Between, before, beyond
By, in, from, off, on, over, of
Until, unto, upon

CHORUS:
Under, underneath, since, up
Like, near, past, throughout, through
With, within, without, instead
Toward, inside, into, to

1. The queen wasn't wild about going through the mud.
2. But the king was interested in the library money.
3. The kids couldn't wait until race day.
4. But the queen wasn't looking forward to it.
5. The king enjoyed being amid the other competitors.
6. They had trouble hearing the announcements on the bullhorn.
7. After the announcements, they used the space porter.
8. The king spoke about grammar during the race.

⭐ Step 2: Find the Object of the Preposition

Highlight the noun or pronoun that answers the question what? after the preposition. *Underline the preposition(s). The number of them is in parentheses after the sentence.* **Hint:** *Only highlight the noun or pronoun and not the adjectives. Both words in a proper noun should be highlighted.*

1. The Grammar Dash is a race through the mud. (1)

2. The queen was concerned about the race being on TV. (1)

3. The Pain Time obstacle requires hanging on monkey bars. (1)

4. Summet Plummets has participants climbing up a 15-foot wall. (1)

5. During your climb, keep a firm grip! (1)

6. At Cage Crawl, you go through a ditch filled with dirty, cold water. (3)

7. The Everest obstacle requires running up a steep, slippery halfpipe. (1)

8. The Fire Walker obstacle makes you run among pits of fire with 4-foot flames. (3)

Activity. *Set up an obstacle course. Try to describe it to your family/friends without using objects of prepositions (OPs) first. Then include the OPs and have a timed competition on your course.*

⭐ Step 3: Label the Prepositions and Objects

Write P above prepositions and OP above the object of the preposition for each sentence. *There may be more than one P and OP per sentence.*

1. The queen didn't want mud on her clothing.

2. Running in the race sounded good to Luke.

3. Walking through fire seemed frightening to Kirk.

4. Ellen said yes without hesitation for the library donation.

5. The queen couldn't have her family participating without her.

6. First aid was available along the course for injured people.

7. Without a doubt, the race was the scariest event of her life.

8. The king and queen were counting on their kids.

Vocabulary Victory! Do you remember what these words mean? *Check Step 1 if you need a reminder.*

morose	The king looked **morose** after taking a phone call.
reverie	"You children have always loved obstacle courses," the queen said in a **reverie**.
encounter	"The next obstacle you'll **encounter** is Pain Time," the director said.

☆ Advanced Guardians Only

Describe a mudder obstacle course of your own, using prepositions and objects of prepostions. *Give your race and obstacles names.*

Race_____

Obstacle #1_____

Description:

Obstacle #2_____

Description:

Obstacle #3_____

Description:

Obstacle #4_____

Description:

Obstacle #5_____

Description:

Mission 19: Update

Dear guardians,

    We found many objects of prepositions attending a rally for word rights. Kirk took the microphone and explained that words also had a right to work. He said that the galaxy needed them, and if they went back to work, we could run the Grammar Dash race as planned.

    Ellen and Luke used your completed mission to lead the OPs back to their positions. They were thrilled to be a part of helping us complete the race. We are so glad we completed the Grammar Dash. Our mother? Not so much.

    Check the solutions we are sending you to make sure you're on track.

Gratefully,

Kirk, Luke, and Ellen English
Guardians of Grammar Galaxy

Step 1 Solutions

On Guard.

1. Which of these is the present participle in the sentence?
   found   lying   shoes
2. Which of these words in the sentence should be hyphenated?
   size-seven   found-lying   in-the-closet
3. What is the object of the preposition in the sentence?
   hers   shoes   closet
4. How should the possessive word in the sentence be written?
   her's   hers   her
5. How should the number in the sentence be written?
   seven   7   11

Review prepositions.

1. The queen wasn't wild about going through the mud.
2. But the king was interested in the library money.
3. The kids couldn't wait until race day.
4. But the queen wasn't looking forward to it.
5. The king enjoyed being amid the other competitors.
6. They had trouble hearing the announcements on the bullhorn.
7. After the announcements, they used the space porter.
8. The king spoke about grammar during the race.

Step 2 Solutions

1. The Grammar Dash is a race through the mud. (1)
2. The queen was concerned about the race being on TV. (1)
3. The Pain Time obstacle requires hanging on monkey bars. (1)
4. Summet Plummets has participants climbing up a 15-foot wall. (1)
5. During your climb, keep a firm grip! (1)
6. At Cage Crawl, you go through a ditch filled with dirty, cold water. (3)
7. The Everest obstacle requires running up a steep, slippery halfpipe. (1)
8. The Fire Walker obstacle makes you run among pits of fire with 4-foot flames. (3)

Step 3 Solutions

                     P   OP
1. The queen didn't want mud on her clothing.
           P   OP   P   OP
2. Running in the race sounded good to Luke.
          P   OP   P   OP
3. Walking through fire seemed frightening to Kirk.
                 P   OP   P   OP
4. Ellen said yes without hesitation for the library donation.
                             P   OP
5. The queen couldn't have her family participating without her.
            P   OP   P   OP
6. First aid was available along the course for injured people.
   P   OP   P   OP
7. Without a doubt, the race was the scariest event of her life.
                        P   OP
8. The king and queen were counting on their kids.

Mission 20: Subjective vs. Objective Pronouns

Dear guardians,

    Have you been talking like a baby? Us have. It's all because pronouns are the subject of a documentary on planet Sentence. To fix it, Father is going to have some pronouns called the object of the documentary.

    That's where you come in. Us need you to tell us which pronouns are subjective, and which are objective. Us are counting on you! Use the information on the next page to help you complete the mission.

Sincerely,

Kirk, Luke, and Ellen English
Guardians of Grammar Galaxy

Subjective vs. Objective Pronouns

Pronouns take the place of other nouns and can be subjective or objective.

Subjective pronouns take the place of subject nouns. They often appear at the beginning of sentences. Subjective pronouns do the action of a sentence or are what is being described. Subjective pronouns are *I*, *we*, *he*, *she*, *it*, *they*, and *you*.

We left right on time.

I am so cold.

Objective pronouns take the place of nouns acting as the direct object, indirect object, or object of the preposition. Objective pronouns include *me*, *us*, *her*, *him*, *them*, *you*, and *it*.

The coach invited *him* to playoffs.

The teacher gave *her* an award.

This spot is just for *us*.

Objective pronouns cannot be used as the subject of a sentence. *You* and *it* may be used as both subjects and objects.

Her was the first girl in line. – incorrect

She was the first girl in line. – correct

You hit *it* too hard. – correct

To remember which pronoun to use with compound subjects or objects (more than one), use only one pronoun. If it sounds wrong, try switching from objective to subjective or vice versa. Use the pronoun *I* or *me* last in compound subjects and objects.

Me and Caleb are going to the store. – check compound subject

Me is going to the store. – incorrect

Caleb and *I* are going to the store. – correct

I'm getting popcorn for *she* and *I*. – check the compound Ops

I'm getting popcorn for *she*. – one pronoun, incorrect

I'm getting popcorn for *I*. – one pronoun, incorrect

I'm getting popcorn for *her* and *me*. – correct

☆ Step 1: On Guard & Identify Subjective Pronouns

On Guard. *Highlight TRUE or FALSE for each statement.*

1. The object of a preposition is a noun or pronoun.   TRUE   FALSE

2. Past participles for irregular verbs vary.   TRUE   FALSE

3. You should use numerals for decimals.   TRUE   FALSE

4. To communicate well, you can choose any synonym for a word from a thesaurus.   TRUE   FALSE

5. The words *blue* and *blew* are the same part of speech.   TRUE   FALSE

Say each of these words in a sentence. *Examples are given.*

trailed – followed	The dolphins **trailed** the ship.
neglecting – failing	My mother wants to know if I've been **neglecting** to brush my teeth.
unrest – conflict	Adding a new guinea pig to the cage caused **unrest**.

221

Identify subjective pronouns. *Read the sentence. For each blank, highlight the subjective pronoun that belongs there. Review the subjective pronouns before answering.* **Hint:** <u>Pronouns are never proper nouns (names)</u>.

1. _____ was using baby talk.
   Luke   him   he

2. _____ and Kirk went to the robotics competition.
   He   Him   King

3. _____ and the queen went shopping.
   She   Her   Ellen

4. _____ had a delicious lunch.
   We   Us   Ellen

5. The king and _____ enjoyed their time at the competition.
   Kirk   him   he

6. Comet and _____ went for a walk.
   Luke   him   he

7. _____ and Cook looked after Luke.
   He   Butler   Him

8. "Comet and _____ had a great time!"
   me   Luke   I

☆ Step 2: Identify the Objective Pronoun

Highlight the objective pronoun that belongs in the blank. *Review the list objective pronouns before answering.*

1. The king and queen didn't know what was wrong with _____.
   Luke   he   him

2. The queen invited Luke to come along with Ellen and _____.
   she   her   they

3. The king invited _____ to the competition with them.
   Luke   him   he

4. Luke asked _____ if he could stay home.
   Father   him   he

5. Ellen heard _____ talking about Luke.
   them   they   Mother

6. When Ellen talked baby talk, the queen worried about _____.
   her   she   Ellen

7. Ellen wanted _____ half of dessert too.
   Mother's   she   her

8. "You can trust Cook with _____," Luke said.
   I   me   Luke

Activity. *This week try to catch your family members using the wrong subjective or objective pronoun. Explain what you've learned and give the correct pronoun for what was said. For example, if your sibling says, "Me and her are going to play," say "She and I are going to play. I learned that She and I are subjective pronouns."*

223

⭐ <u>Step 3: Write the Correct Pronoun</u>
Write a correct subjective or objective pronoun in the blank, using story 20. *Read the sentence. Determine if the missing word is the subject and takes a subjective pronoun or is an object (direct, indirect, or OP) and takes an objective pronoun.* **Hint:** <u>Do not use proper nouns</u>.

1. _____ and Kirk left for the robotics competition.

2. The queen took _____ shopping and out for lunch.

3. Luke wanted to stay home with _____ and Cook.

4. "She and _____ could take Luke with us," the queen said.

5. "_____ could also take him with us," the king said.

6. "Comet and _____ are going for a walk," Luke said.

7. "Don't worry about _____," Luke added.

8. _____ split a dessert after lunch.

Vocabulary Victory! Do you remember what these words mean? *Check Step 1 if you need a reminder.*

assent	"I won't give my **assent**," the king said.
apprised	The Prime Minister promised to keep the king **apprised** of the bill's progress.
replete	The Internet was **replete** with ads discussing the unfairness words faced with spelling.

☆ Advanced Guardians Only

If we could convince the documentary team on planet Sentence to interview your family, what would they think was most interesting about you? *Write about your family's unique history, hobbies, or habits below, being careful to use subjective and objective pronouns correctly.*

_____
_____
_____
_____
_____
_____
_____
_____
_____
_____
_____
_____
_____
_____
_____
_____
_____
_____
_____
_____

Mission 20: Update

Dear guardian friends,

We aren't using baby talk anymore! With your help, we were able to have some pronouns officially titled the object, and not the subject, of a documentary.

Even though we achieved our goal, watch for some pronouns still being used incorrectly. Just between us, a lot of people mix up these pronouns.

Some of your families are so interesting that the film crew wants to interview you! You may be hearing from them.

We have included the solutions to your mission.

Sincerely,

Kirk, Luke, and Ellen English

Guardians of Grammar Galaxy

Step 1 Solutions

On Guard.

1. The object of a preposition is a noun or pronoun.   TRUE   FALSE
2. Past participles for irregular verbs vary.   TRUE   FALSE
3. You should use numerals for decimals.   TRUE   FALSE
4. To communicate well, you can choose any synonym for a word from a thesaurus.   TRUE   FALSE
5. The words *blue* and *blew* are the same part of speech.   TRUE   FALSE

Step 2 Solutions

1. The king and queen didn't know what was wrong with _____.
   Luke   he   him

2. The queen invited Luke to come along with Ellen and _____.
   she   her   they

3. The king invited _____ to the competition with them.
   Luke   him   he

4. Luke asked _____ if he could stay home.
   Father   him   he

5. Ellen heard _____ talking about Luke.
   them   they   Mother

6. When Ellen talked baby talk, the queen worried about _____.
   her   she   Ellen

7. Ellen wanted _____ half of dessert too.
   Mother's   she   her

8. "You can trust Cook with _____," Luke said.
   I   me   Luke

Step 3 Solutions

1. He and Kirk left for the robotics competition.

2. The queen took her shopping and out for lunch.

3. Luke wanted to stay home with him and Cook.

4. "She and I could take Luke with us," the queen said.

5. "We could also take him with us," the king said.

6. "Comet and I are going for a walk," Luke said.

7. "Don't worry about me," Luke added. – us is also acceptable

8. They split a dessert after lunch.

228

Mission 21: Interrogative Pronouns

Dear guardians,

What are you doing today? Who has time for a mission? You may have noticed that you are saying *who*, *what*, *which*, *whom*, and *whose* a lot more than normal. We believe that's because these interrogative pronouns are being interviewed for a documentary on planet Sentence.

That's where we're going now. Please help us identify these interrogative pronouns, so we can ask to have them excused from the filming. Who's the greatest for helping us? You are!

We're including the information you need on the next page.

Sincerely,

Kirk and Ellen English
Guardians of Grammar Galaxy

Interrogative Pronouns

The five interrogative pronouns are used to ask questions. They are *who, whom, what,* and *which*. The possessive pronoun *whose* may also be used as an interrogative pronoun. The answer to the question is the antecedent (noun replaced by the interrogative pronoun). But it may be unknown.

Who took my pen?

Whose shoe is this*?*

What day is it?

Who, whom, and *whose* are used to ask questions about people. **What and which are** used to ask questions about people or things.

Who is used when the answer is the subject of the sentence.

Whom is used when the answer is a direct object, indirect object, or the object of a preposition. Note that *whom* generally isn't used in conversation or informal writing.

Whom was hit by the ball?

The suffix *-ever* may be added to interrogative pronouns to show surprise or confusion.

Whatever did you think you were doing?

230

⭐ Step 1: On Guard & Find the Interrogative Pronouns

On Guard. *Answer the following questions or answer verbally for your teacher.*

1. What is the difference between a subjective and an objective pronoun?

2. What is an object of the preposition?

3. What is a participle?

4. What are two cases when numbers should be spelled out?

5. What are three words you would use to express shades of meaning for a good mood?

Say each of these words in a sentence. *Examples are given.*

donned – put on	I **donned** my coat before Mom could remind me.
bickering – arguing	My parents don't like **bickering**.
mimicking – imitating	I can't stand it when people are **mimicking** me.

Find interrogative pronouns. *Read the sentence. Highlight the interrogative pronouns.* **Hint:** <u>*There may be more than one*</u>.

1. What was the problem at the spaceball game?

2. Who was playing first?

3. "Whatever do you boys think you are doing?" the queen asked.

4. The king asked which player was up to bat.

5. "Who is on first and what is his batting average?" the king asked.

6. *I wonder what is going on*, Ellen thought.

7. Ellen was glad no one asked whose frozen lemonade she was eating.

8. Kirk and Ellen wondered whom to speak with and what they would say.

⭐ Step 2: Choose Who or Whom

Highlight whether who or whom should be used in the sentence.
Assume this is formal writing. **Hint:** *Who is used when the antecedent is a subject and whom is used when the antecedent is an object.*

1. The kids started their business letter with "To _____ it may concern."
   who   whom

2. A receptionist greeted them. "With _____ is your appointment?"
   who   whom

3. The kids wanted to know _____ decided to interview interrogative pronouns.
   who   whom

4. When they arrived, they asked _____ had read their letter.
   who   whom

5. They asked _____ they had interviewed so far.
   who   whom

Activity. *Watch Abbott & Costello's "Who's On First." See GrammarGalaxyBooks.com/RedStar for a link.*

☆ Step 3: Write the Interrogative Pronoun That Makes Sense

Write the interrogative pronoun that belongs in the blank, using story 21.

1. The king didn't know _____ was on first.

2. Kirk thought he knew _____ program it was.

3. "_____ do you think you're doing?" the queen asked.

4. Ellen didn't know _____ was going on.

5. Kirk wanted to know _____ was going with him.

6. Ellen asked Luke _____ his favorite sister was.

7. Kirk and Ellen were thankful the king told them _____ article to read in the guidebook.

8. Kirk said _____ was on third base.

Vocabulary Victory! Do you remember what these words mean? *Check Step 1 if you need a reminder.*

donned	The queen **donned** her sunglasses as their seats were in the sun.
bickering	"What are you two **bickering** about?" the queen c
mimicking	"Why are you **mimicking** me," the queen asked.

⭐ <u>Advanced Guardians Only</u>

Write questions for your family members to answer. *The documentary team is interested in talking with your family, but they need your help to come up with the questions to ask about your family's unique history, hobbies, or habits. Use each of the five interrogatory pronouns at least once.*

1. _____

2. _____

3. _____

4. _____

5. _____

6. _____

7. _____

8. _____

Mission 21: Update

Dear guardians,

What did you do? Don't worry. We're just excited to thank you for helping us. Using your completed missions, we were able to get the interrogative pronouns excused from the documentary. The documentary team loved the questions you wrote for them to ask your family. That will save them a lot of time in interviews.

You worked so quickly that Kirk and Ellen were able to get back to the stadium. The whole family enjoyed a real spaceball game with big-name players.

Thank you! Please check the solutions to this mission, so you know for sure what you're doing.

Sincerely,

Kirk, Luke, and Ellen English
Guardians of Grammar Galaxy

Step 1 Solutions

On Guard.

1. **What is the difference between a subjective and an objective pronoun?** Subjective pronouns take the place of subject nouns. Objective pronouns take the place of nouns acting as the direct object, indirect object, or object of the preposition.
2. **What is an object of the preposition?** The noun or pronoun at the end of a prepositional phrase.
3. **What is a participle?** Participles are verb forms that can be used as part of a multi-word verb, as adjectives, or as nouns.
4. **What are two cases when numbers should be spelled out?** Numbers one to nine; numbers at the beginning of a sentence, when numbers appear next to each other in the text; in dialogue or quotes.
5. **What are three words you would use to express shades of meaning for a good mood?** Glad, happy, ecstatic (answers will vary)

Find interrogative pronouns.

1. What was the problem at the spaceball game?

2. Who was playing first?

3. "Whatever do you boys think you are doing?" the queen asked.

4. The king asked which player was up to bat?

5. "Who is on first and what is his batting average?" the king asked.

6. *I wonder what is going on*, Ellen thought.

7. Ellen was glad no one asked whose frozen lemonade she was eating.

8. Kirk and Ellen wondered whom to speak with and what they would say.

Step 2 Solutions

1. The kids started their business letter with "To _____ it may concern."
   who   whom

2. A receptionist greeted them. "With _____ is your appointment?"
   who   whom

3. The kids wanted to know _____ decided to interview interrogative pronouns.
   who   whom

4. When they arrived, they asked _____ had read their letter.
   who   whom

5. They asked _____ they had interviewed so far.
   who   whom

Step 3 Solutions

1. The king didn't know <u>who</u> was on first.

2. Kirk thought he knew <u>whose</u> program it was.

3. "<u>What</u> do you think you're doing?" the queen asked.

4. Ellen didn't know <u>what</u> was going on.

5. Kirk wanted to know <u>who</u> was going with him.

6. Ellen asked Luke <u>who</u> his favorite sister was.

7. Kirk and Ellen were thankful the king told them <u>which</u> article to read in the guidebook.

8. Kirk said <u>Whom</u> was on third base.

Mission 22: Demonstrative Pronouns

Dear guardians,

You won't believe what just happened to us! We were told that a group of words making noise during Father's speech on planet Sentence was dangerous. We were then locked in a room, supposedly for our safety. We learned that these men were working with the Gremlin. And it turns out that the words weren't violent demonstrators; they're demonstrative pronouns.

The words *this*, *that*, *these* and *those* are demonstrative pronouns that take the place of nouns when used alone. When used to describe nouns, they're demonstrative adjectives and are used for emphasis.

Kirk thought it would be a good idea to have you identify these demonstrators, so we won't be afraid of them in the future. That's what this mission is all about. Thank you for serving so faithfully!

Sincerely,

Kirk, Luke, and Ellen English
Guardians of Grammar Galaxy

☆ Step 1: On Guard & Identify Demonstrative Pronouns & Adjectives

On Guard. *Highlight TRUE or FALSE for each statement.*

1. <u>Whom</u> should always be used in conversation and informal writing.　　　TRUE　FALSE

2. Subjective pronouns include *I, he*, and *she*.　　　TRUE　FALSE

3. In the sentence <u>A box of books arrived today.</u> *box* is the object of the preposition.　　　TRUE　FALSE

4. In the sentence <u>I looked at the faded picture.</u> *faded* is a participle used as an adjective.　　　TRUE　FALSE

5. When numbers appear next to each other in the text, one number should be spelled out.　　　TRUE　FALSE

Say each of these words in a sentence. *Examples are given.*

proactive – act before	I like to be **proactive** and get my work done early.
resolutely – determinedly	The monkey at the zoo held onto its banana **resolutely**.
discern – determine	I can't **discern** whether I will like this book or not.

Identify demonstrative pronouns and demonstrative adjectives.
Read the sentence. Highlight the demonstrative pronouns and adjectives.

1. Luke didn't know what to say for this speech.

2. Kirk didn't want to help him with that.

3. The queen told Luke to use just those thoughts in his speech.

4. That group of demonstrators was distracting to the king.

5. "I don't know what to think about this," the king said.

6. "Those words aren't safe!" the guards warned.

7. "These are not my security guards," the king said.

8. "That was a scary experience!" Luke said.

⭐ Step 2: Differentiate Between Demonstrative Pronouns and Adjectives

Highlight the demonstrative pronouns and adjectives in each sentence. *Write PRO above demonstrative pronouns and ADJ above demonstrative adjectives.* **Hint:** *Demonstrative adjectives are usually followed by a noun.*

1. "These citizens deserve a visit," the king said.

2. "I'm looking forward to this trip," the king said.

3. Speaking—that was the part Luke wasn't looking forward to.

4. The queen helped Luke put those thoughts into a short speech.

5. That made him feel more confident about talking onstage.

6. That alphabet-soup joke went over well.

7. Those words to the left started the problem.

8. Luke devised a plan to get past those guards.

Activity. *Make a video demonstrating your house for the documentary team. Count how many times you used demonstrative pronouns in your video.*

⭐ <u>Step 3: Rewrite Sentences with Demonstrative Pronouns or Adjectives</u>

Rewrite the sentences using either a demonstrative pronoun (PRO) or demonstrative adjective (ADJ) as indicated in parentheses.

1. No one understood what the demonstrators were saying. (ADJ)

   _____

   _____

2. "Why are you doing an evacuation?" the king asked. (PRO)

   _____

   _____

3. "What we are doing is standard operating procedure," a guard answered. (PRO)

   _____

   _____

4. "Are the shoes by the door yours?" one guard asked Luke. (ADJ)

   _____

   _____

5. "No, the shoes on my feet are mine," Luke answered, pointing. (PRO)

   _____

   _____

Vocabulary Victory! Do you remember what these words mean? *Check Step 1 if you need a reminder.*

proactive	We need to be **proactive** and visit before there's a problem.
resolutely	"Luke, I don't want to tell you and have you copy Kirk said **resolutely**.
discern	When he couldn't **discern** what the issue was, he struggled to continue.

☆ <u>Advanced Guardians Only</u>

Create positive signs for demonstrators to hold, using demonstrative pronouns and adjectives. *Write what is going well and what there is to be grateful for. For example, This planet is beautiful!*

Mission 22: Update

Dear guardians,

　　This is one of your best missions to date! All of your missions are great, but we wanted to use a demonstrative pronoun.

　　We gave the signs you made to *this*, *that*, *these*, and *those*, and they loved them! The next time we visit planet Sentence, they'll be demonstrating in a positive way.

　　We are including the solutions to your mission for you to review.

Sincerely,

Kirk, Luke, and Ellen English
Guardians of Grammar Galaxy

Step 1 Solutions

On Guard.

1. <u>Whom</u> should always be used in conversation and informal writing.   TRUE   FALSE
2. Subjective pronouns include I, he, and she.   TRUE   FALSE
3. In the sentence <u>A box of books arrived today.</u> box is the object of the preposition.   TRUE   FALSE
4. In the sentence <u>I looked at the faded picture.</u> faded is a participle used as an adjective.   TRUE   FALSE
5. When numbers appear next to each other in the text, one number should be spelled out.   TRUE   FALSE

Identify demonstrative pronouns and adjectives.

1. Luke didn't know what to say for this speech.

2. Kirk didn't want to help him with that.

3. The queen told Luke to use just those thoughts in his speech.

4. That group of demonstrators was distracting to the king.

5. "I don't know what to think about this," the king said.

6. "Those words aren't safe!" the guards warned.

7. "These are not my security guards," the king said.

8. "That was a scary experience!" Luke said.

Step 2 Solutions

   ADJ
1. "These citizens deserve a visit," the king said.

         ADJ
2. "I'm looking forward to this trip," the king said.

      PRO
3. Speaking—that was the part Luke wasn't looking forward to.

          ADJ
4. The queen helped Luke put those thoughts into a short speech.

  PRO
5. That made him feel more confident about talking onstage.

 ADJ
6. That alphabet-soup joke went over well.

 ADJ
7. Those words to the left started the problem.

         ADJ
8. Luke devised a plan to get past those guards.

Step 3 Solutions - demonstrative pronouns and adjectives are underlined; answers may vary

1. No one understood what <u>those</u> demonstrators were saying. (ADJ)

2. "Why are you doing <u>that</u>?" the king asked. (PRO)

3. "<u>This</u> is standard operating procedure," a guard answered. (PRO)

4. "Are <u>those</u> shoes by the door yours?" one guard asked Luke. (ADJ)

5. "No, <u>these</u> shoes are mine," Luke answered, pointing. (PRO)

246

Mission 23: Reflexive Pronouns

Dear guardians,

It's embarrassing to admit, but we have been hitting ourselves. If you yourselves have experienced this too, don't be ashamed. The problem is reflexive pronouns. We ourselves think they are being given a physical exam that includes a reflex test. When they respond reflexively, we're hitting ourselves.

We plan to travel to planet Sentence to have the reflexive pronouns excused from the documentary. But we can't accomplish this mission ourselves. We need you to identify the reflexive pronouns who are ready to get physicals. We can then have their physicals cancelled, and we can get back to enjoying ourselves again. We're including the information you need for the mission on the next page.

Sincerely,

Kirk, Luke, and Ellen English
Guardians of Grammar Galaxy

Reflexive Pronouns

Reflexive pronouns are pronouns that end in *-self* or *-selves*. Reflexive pronouns include *myself, oneself, ourselves, yourself, yourselves, himself, herself, itself*, and *themselves*.

Reflexive is Latin for reflect. Reflexive pronouns are direct and indirect objects that reflect back to the subject.

I hit *myself* with a hammer. – direct object
I gave *myself* a haircut. – indirect object

Reflexive pronouns cannot serve as subjects. A common error is to include a reflexive pronoun in a compound subject. To detect the error, remove the other subject from the sentence.

Joe and myself are going fishing this weekend – incorrect
Myself is going fishing this weekend. – subject removed, incorrect
Joe and I are going fishing this weekend – correct

Another common error is to use a reflexive pronoun as an indirect object that does not match the subject.

You can give Jane and *myself* the money later. – incorrect
(*myself* doesn't match the subject *you*)
You can give Jane and me the money later. – correct
You can give me the money later and I'll buy myself a treat. – correct
(*myself* matches the second subject *I* in *I'll*)

Reflexive pronouns may also be used as intensive pronouns. They intensify or emphasize the subject or antecedent to show that someone else did not do the action. Intensive pronouns may be removed from a sentence without changing the meaning.

I made the pie crust *myself*.
We *ourselves* moved the furniture.

☆ Step 1: On Guard & Find the Reflexive Pronoun

On Guard. *Highlight the correct answer for each statement.*

1. Which word is a demonstrative pronoun?
   this   their

2. Which word is an interrogative pronoun?
   why   what

3. Which pronoun can be used as an object of a preposition?
   her   she

4. Which word can be used as an object of a preposition?
   tree   speak

5. Which word can be used a participle?
   ugly   driving

Say each of these words in a sentence. *Examples are given.*

errant – wayward	An **errant** paper airplane hit me in the nose.
commended – praised	My friend **commended** me for not getting sick on the roller coaster.
tremulously – tremblingly	The baby bird sat on my palm **tremulously**.

Find the reflexive pronoun. *Read the sentence. Highlight the reflexive pronoun if there is one.*

1. The queen and kids kept hitting themselves as they played tennis.

2. The king himself wondered what was going on.

3. He kept hitting tennis balls to them anyway.

4. They wanted to quit, and he knew he couldn't play by himself.

5. Cook had created the vegetable dish recipe herself.

6. She would have blamed herself if she had made the family sick.

7. "I myself did not eat the vegetables," the king said.

8. When the king hit himself, he knew something was wrong.

⭐ <u>Step 2: Find the Incorrect Reflexive Pronouns</u>
Highlight reflexive pronouns used incorrectly in the sentences.
Note: <u>Sentences may contain no errors.</u>

1. The king blamed himself for making fun of his family.

2. "Kirk and myself will lead the mission," Luke said.

3. "No, Kirk and myself will lead the mission," Ellen objected.

4. "I myself am in charge of the mission," the king said.

5. "You can each report to myself," the king added.

6. He encouraged themselves to leave immediately.

7. Luke knew he couldn't complete the mission himself.

8. "You can count on Luke, Ellen, and myself," Kirk said.

Activity. *Do any of the following things you can do as* **myself** *using good grammar. Ignore those you can't.*

I will make myself a snack.
My teacher and myself will skip school today.
I'm going to give myself a neck massage.
I'm going to do 20 jumping jacks myself.
My teacher is going to give myself $5.

⭐ Step 3: Rewrite the Sentences Using Reflexive Pronouns Correctly

Rewrite the sentence so it is grammatically correct, removing or replacing reflexive pronouns as necessary.

1. "You can't blame myself for your lack of practice," the king said.

_____

_____

2. "You have no one but ourselves to blame."

_____

_____

3. "Ellen and myself ate the vegetables," the queen said.

_____

_____

4. He gave themselves a mission.

_____

_____

5. "Me myself think it's doable," Kirk said.

_____

_____

Vocabulary Victory! Do you remember what these words mean? *Check Step 1 if you need a reminder.*

assent	"I won't give my **assent**," the king said.
apprised	The Prime Minister promised to keep the king **apprised** of the bill's progress.
replete	The Internet was **replete** with ads discussing the unfairness words faced with spelling.

☆ <u>Advanced Guardians Only</u>
Write about a time you were hurt trying to do something yourself.
Use a reflexive pronoun at least three times.

_____

_____

_____

_____

_____

_____

_____

_____

_____

_____

_____

_____

_____

_____

_____

_____

_____

_____

Mission 23: Update

Dear guardians,

     Our bruises are healing, thanks to you! Because you helped us identify reflexive pronouns, we were able to get their physicals cancelled. We are no longer hitting ourselves. And we thank you for the warning about hurting ourselves by trying to do things ourselves. We'll ask for help.

     We are including the solutions to this mission. Don't hit yourself if you didn't get something right. Grammar, like tennis, takes lots of practice.

Sincerely,

Kirk, Luke, and Ellen English

Guardians of Grammar Galaxy

Step 1 Solutions
On Guard.
1. Which word is a demonstrative pronoun?
   this   their
2. Which word is an interrogative pronoun?
   why   what
3. Which pronoun can be used as an object of a preposition?
   her   she
4. Which word can be used as an object of a preposition?
   tree   speak
5. Which word can be used a participle?
   ugly   driving

Find the reflexive pronoun.
1. The queen and kids kept hitting themselves as they played tennis.
2. The king himself wondered what was going on.
3. He kept hitting tennis balls to them anyway.
4. They wanted to quit, and he knew he couldn't play by himself.
5. Cook had created the vegetable dish recipe herself.
6. She would have blamed herself if she had made the family sick.
7. "I myself did not eat the vegetables," the king said.
8. When the king hit himself, he knew something was wrong.

Step 2 Solutions
1. The king blamed himself for making fun of his family.
2. "Kirk and myself will lead the mission," Luke said.
3. "No, Kirk and myself will lead the mission," Ellen objected.
4. "I myself am in charge of the mission," the king said.
5. "You can each report to myself," the king added.
6. He encouraged themselves to leave immediately.
7. Luke knew he couldn't complete the mission himself.
8. "You can count on Luke, Ellen, and myself," Kirk said.

Activity.
I will make myself a snack.
My teacher and myself will skip school today. -incorrect
I'm going to give myself a neck massage.
I'm going to do 20 jumping jacks myself.
My teacher is going to give myself $5. -incorrect

Step 3 Solutions – changes are underlined
1. "You can't blame me for your lack of practice," the king said.

2. "You have no one but yourself to blame."

3. "Ellen and I ate the vegetables," the queen said.

4. He gave them a mission.

5. "I myself think it's doable," Kirk said

Mission 24: Indefinite Pronouns

Dear guardians,

      Sometimes less are more. Oops! We know that's wrong, but we can't change it until you help us complete this mission. Indefinite pronouns' paperwork is being incorrectly stamped as singular or plural. We need you to mark the paperwork correctly. Then we can start speaking correctly. And maybe our family will get along better. For now, someone aren't happy!

Sincerely,

Kirk, Luke, and Ellen English

Guardians of Grammar Galaxy

P.S. Father told us to say it isn't right to say that someone aren't happy. We don't know if he doesn't want us sharing personal information, or if he means grammar. Either way, someone will be happier when your mission is complete. We are including information about indefinite pronouns on the next page to help you.

Indefinite Pronouns

Indefinite pronouns are pronouns that do not refer to specific nouns. To have subject-verb agreement with indefinite pronouns, learn which pronouns are singular and which are plural.

Indefinite pronouns ending in -one, -body, and -thing are always singular and take a singular verb.

Someone is in my seat! (singular verb)

Everybody has a place at the table. (singular verb)

Everything is beautiful! (singular verb)

Other singular indefinite pronouns include *another*, *each*, *either*, *much*, *little*, *neither*, and *other*.

Either is fine. (singular verb)

Much has been said about the topic. (singular verb)

The indefinite pronouns *both*, *few*, *many*, *others*, and *several* **are always plural.**

Few are able to pass the test. (plural verb)

Several have told me about the park. (plural verb)

Other indefinite pronouns are singular or plural depending on how they are used. They include *all*, *any*, *more*, *most*, and *some*.

When used with a noun that can be counted, use a plural verb.

Some of the quarters are on the floor. (quarters can be counted; plural)

When used with a noun that cannot be counted, use a singular verb.

Some of the flour is on the floor. (flour can't be counted; singular)

When used to describe a noun (rather than standing alone), the words *any, each, few, some, many, much,* and *most* **are indefinite adjectives. Verb agreement is with the noun.**

Any player who breaks the rules will be eliminated. (singular verb)

Some kids prefer to work alone. (plural verb)

⭐ Step 1: On Guard & Find the Indefinite Pronoun

On Guard. *Answer the questions or answer verbally for your teacher.*

1. What is an example of a reflexive pronoun?

2. What is an example of a demonstrative pronoun?

3. What is an example of an interrogative pronoun?

4. What is an example of a subjective pronoun?

5. What is an example of an object of the preposition?

Say each of these words in a sentence. *Examples are given.*

purged – removed	We **purged** all our baby stuff and then our baby brother was born.
streamline – simplify	Mom says we need to **streamline** our morning routine.
deteriorate – worsen	My grandma tries to save plants, but they usually **deteriorate**.

Find the indefinite pronoun. *Read the sentence. Highlight any indefinite pronouns you find.*

1. The queen removed everything from her closet.

2. The king didn't want anything taken from his closet.

3. The queen said most of the king's clothes weren't being worn.

4. "Some of these clothes I've worn," the king protested.

5. "Several of these suits are covered in dust," the queen retorted.

6. "You've worn few of them," she added.

7. "Someone needs to focus on her own closet," the king joked.

8. He promised to go through all of his clothes later.

⭐ Step 2: Choose a Singular or Plural Verb

Highlight the verb that belongs in the blank. *Determine whether the indefinite pronoun or adjective is singular or plural. Then choose a verb to match.*

1. All of the queen's conversations _____ about minimalism.
   is   are

2. She says everyone _____ talking about it.
   is   are

3. The king thinks neither _____ good—too much or too little.
   is   are

4. Everybody _____ an opinion on the topic.
   has   have

5. Others _____ an idea of how much is enough.
   has   have

6. But most of her clothes _____ unworn.
   is   are

7. Any shirt that _____ damage will be given away.
   has   have

8. But some women _____ more clothes than others.
   want   wants

Activity. *With your parent's help, purge some things you don't need or use. Try to use as many of this mission's indefinite pronouns correctly as you can while you work. How many did you use?*

⭐ Step 3: Rewrite the Sentences Using the Correct Verb

Write the sentence correctly using a singular or plural verb to match the indefinite pronoun. *The sentence may be correct as written.* **Hint:** *Underline book titles.*

1. I'm so motivated from reading *Less Are More*.

   _____

   _____

2. Anything you don't use or need are too much.

   _____

   _____

3. Each of us is entitled to our own opinion.

   _____

   _____

4. Everybody have loved this book.

   _____

   _____

5. Some dresses is in boxes to go to charity.

   _____

   _____

Vocabulary Victory! Do you remember what these words mean? *Check Step 1 if you need a reminder.*

purged	When was the last time you **purged** something?
streamline	It feels so good to **streamline** your closet.
deteriorate	Your mother's grammar wouldn't **deteriorate** just because she was excited about minimalism.

☆ Advanced Guardians Only

Write your opinion about something that affects your family. *Use a singular indefinite pronoun, a plural indefinite pronoun, and an indefinite adjective with matching verbs in your writing. Highlight them.*

264

Mission 24: Update

Dear guardian friends,

   We are thrilled to report that indefinite pronouns no longer have to have their paperwork stamped. And those words that were marked singular or plural have been correctly marked, thanks to you!

   We are also happy to report that the someone we mentioned in our letter is much happier now that everyone agrees less is more. Father says we shouldn't be more specific than that. But we can be specific in giving you the solutions to this mission. Thanks so much for your hard work!

Sincerely,

Kirk, Luke, and Ellen English
Guardians of Grammar Galaxy

Step 1 Solutions

On Guard.

1. **What is an example of a reflexive pronoun?** myself, oneself, ourselves, yourself, yourselves, himself, herself, itself, themselves
2. **What is an example of a demonstrative pronoun?** this, that, these, those
3. **What is an example of an interrogative pronoun?** *who, whom, what, which*
4. **What is an example of a subjective pronoun?** *I, we, he, she, it, they, you*
5. **What is an example of an object of the preposition?** Answers will vary.

Find the indefinite pronouns.

1. The queen removed everything from her closet.
2. The king didn't want anything taken from his closet.
3. The queen said most of the king's clothes weren't being worn.
4. "Some of these clothes I've worn," the king protested.
5. "Several of these suits are covered in dust," the queen retorted.
6. "You've worn few of them," she added.
7. "Someone needs to focus on her own closet," the king joked.
8. He promised to go through all of his clothes later.

Step 2 Solutions

1. All of the queen's conversations _____ about minimalism.
    is   are
2. She says everyone _____ talking about it.
    is   are
3. The king thinks neither _____ good—too much or too little.
    is   are
4. Everybody _____ an opinion on the topic.
    has   have
5. Others _____ an idea of how much is enough.
    has   have
6. But most of her clothes _____ unworn.
    is   are
7. Any shirt that _____ damage will be given away.
    has   have
8. But some women _____ more clothes than others.
    want   wants

Step 3 Solutions – changed are underlined

1. I'm so motivated from reading *Less Is More.*
2. Anything you don't use or need is too much.
3. Each of us is entitled to our own opinion. (correct as written)
4. Everybody has loved this book.
5. Some dresses are in boxes to go to charity.

Mission 25: Dependent vs. Independent Clauses

Dear guardians,

If we don't go to planet Sentence soon. We know that doesn't make sense. You too may be having trouble communicating. Here's why. The dependent clauses have declared their independence.

As soon as we get there. Sorry about that. We'd like to show the dependent clauses a copy of their Constitution. It clearly states that they cannot claim independence. In order to do that. Sorry again. We need your help! Please identify the dependent clauses that we need to meet. We've provided the information you need for this mission on the next page.

Sincerely,

Kirk, Luke, and Ellen English
Guardians of Grammar Galaxy

Dependent and Independent Clauses

A dependent clause (also called a subordinate clause) requires an independent clause to make sense. An independent clause can stand alone as a complete sentence.

After we had dinner (dependent clause)
we went to a movie (independent clause)

When a subordinating conjunction joins dependent and independent clauses, a complex sentence is formed. Dependent clauses with a subordinating conjunction at the beginning of a sentence are normally followed by a comma.

After we had dinner, we went to a movie. (complex sentence)

See the chart with common subordinating conjunctions below.

Common Subordinating Conjunctions		
after	in order (that)	when
although	now that	whenever
as	once	where
as soon as	since	wherever
because	so that	whether
before	than	while
even if	that	why
even though	though	
how	till	
if	unless	
in case	until	

☆ Step 1: On Guard & Identify the Dependent Clauses

On Guard. *Highlight TRUE or FALSE for each question.*

1. Indefinite pronouns ending in -one, -body, and -thing are always plural. TRUE FALSE

2. Reflexive pronouns are direct and indirect objects that reflect back to the subject. TRUE FALSE

3. When used before nouns, demonstrative pronouns are adjectives. TRUE FALSE

4. The possessive pronoun *whose* is not an interrogative pronoun. TRUE FALSE

5. Objective pronouns cannot be used as the subject of the sentence. TRUE FALSE

Say each of these words in a sentence. *Examples are given.*

exasperated – frustrated	I was **exasperated** with the fly that kept landing on my nose.
altercation – fight	My dad secretly likes it when there is an **altercation** in hockey.
peeved – annoyed	I was **peeved** when the faucet kept dripping all night.

Identify the dependent clauses. *Read the sentence. Highlight the dependent clause you find in each.* **Hint:** *Look for subordinating conjunctions.*

1. Ellen wanted to say, "When it was time to watch a movie, Amy sat next to Cher and talked to her only."

2. She also wanted to say, "After the movie was over, Amy still kept me out of the conversation."

3. She wanted to add, "Because Amy didn't let me talk to Cher, the party wasn't much fun."

4. She tried to tell the queen, "If you don't understand what I'm saying, how can I talk about it?"

5. "Because it's Saturday," Luke tried to say, "I don't have schoolwork to do."

6. "Although I discovered my computer had a virus," Kirk announced and meant to continue, "I was able to fix it quickly."

7. "I can explain if you want me to tell you about the computer virus," Kirk meant to say.

8. "What will happen now that the clauses are free?" Kirk meant to ask.

☆ Step 2: Mark Clauses as Dependent or Independent
Read each statement and highlight whether it is a dependent or independent clause. *Note:* <u>Dependent clauses require an independent clause to make sense.</u>

1. Unless we do something right away.
   dependent   independent

2. We have to get your mother and sister in here.
   dependent   independent

3. Before you say anything.
   dependent   independent

4. Although I understand what a dependent clause is.
   dependent   independent

5. Even though this is helpful information.
   dependent   independent

6. That's simple.
   dependent   independent

7. When she didn't answer.
   dependent   independent

8. We have to put a stop to this immediately!
   dependent   independent

Activity. *Speak to your family using dependent clauses only. For example, say "After dinner..." How long does it take them to notice that you aren't speaking in complete sentences? Explain what you've learned about dependent and independent clauses.*

271

☆ Step 3: Write Complete Sentences out of Dependent Clauses

Add an independent clause to the dependent clause to form a complete sentence that makes sense. *Hint: Remember to add a comma after a dependent clause at the beginning of a sentence and capitalize the first word.*

1. when I have a problem with a friend

_____

_____

2. if I feel left out

_____

_____

3. before I knew how to handle it

_____

_____

4. unless it's been a repeated problem

_____

_____

5. even though my parent isn't a kid

_____

_____

Vocabulary Victory! Do you remember what these words mean? *Check Step 1 if you need a reminder.*

exasperated	"I know, Mother!" Ellen said, **exasperated**.
altercation	I recall a time when you were having a physical **altercation** with Max.
peeved	"Don't you understand?" Ellen said, clearly **peeved**.

☆ Advanced Guardians Only

Write to an adult family member about a problem you're having, using at least <u>three different subordinating conjunctions</u>. *Highlight them.*

_____

_____

_____

_____

_____

_____

_____

_____

_____

_____

_____

_____

_____

_____

_____

_____

_____

_____

_____

_____

_____

_____

_____

_____

_____

Mission 25: Update

Dear guardians,

If you hadn't completed your mission when you did, we think we would be having a lot of conflict on planet English. Fortunately, we used the work that you did to set up meetings with dependent clauses. We showed them that they can't be legally independent. But we also explained that working with independent clauses is a good thing. Otherwise, they cause confusion.

I (Ellen) feel a lot better after talking with Mother. Talking over problems with parents or other family members is a good idea. Thankfully, we're all understanding one another a lot better now. We hope you are too! Be sure to check your mission answers against the solutions we're sending you.

Sincerely,

Kirk, Luke, and Ellen English

Guardians of Grammar Galaxy

Step 1 Solutions

On Guard.

1.	Indefinite pronouns ending in -one, -body, and -thing are always plural.	TRUE	FALSE
2.	Reflexive pronouns are direct and indirect objects that reflect back to the subject.	TRUE	FALSE
3.	When used before nouns, *this*, *that*, *these*, and *those* are adjectives.	TRUE	FALSE
4.	The possessive pronoun *whose* is not an interrogative pronoun.	TRUE	FALSE
5.	Objective pronouns cannot be used as the subject of the sentence.	TRUE	FALSE

Identify the dependent clauses.

1. Ellen wanted to say, "When it was time to watch a movie, Amy sat next to Cher and talked to her only."
2. She also wanted to say, "After the movie was over, Amy still kept me out of the conversation."
3. She wanted to add, "Because Amy didn't let me talk to Cher, the party wasn't much fun."
4. She tried to tell the queen, "If you don't understand what I'm saying, how can I talk about it?"
5. "Because it's Saturday," Luke tried to say, "I don't have schoolwork to do."
6. "Although I discovered my computer had a virus," Kirk announced and meant to continue, "I was able to fix it quickly."
7. "I can explain if you want me to tell you about the computer virus," Kirk meant to say.
8. "What will happen now that the clauses are free?" Kirk meant to ask.

Step 2 Solutions

1. Unless we do something right away.
   dependent   independent

2. We have to get your mother and sister in here.
   dependent   independent

3. Before you say anything.
   dependent   independent

4. Although I understand what a dependent clause is.
   dependent   independent

5. Even though this is helpful information.
   dependent   independent

6. That's simple.
   dependent   independent

7. When she didn't answer.
   dependent   independent

8. We have to put a stop to this immediately!
   dependent   independent

Step 3 Solutions – answers will vary

Mission 26: Colons & Semicolons

Attention guardians:

If you've looked at any writing lately; you'll notice a lot of incorrect colons and semicolons; In fact, we seem to be using them whether we want to or not: At least you'll see the problem with them:

There are just too many of them! We plan to talk to Inky: Remember her from Contraction and Abbreviation Nation? She is adding colons and semicolons where they don't belong: We need your help to remove them if they're incorrect; Ellen hopes to convince Inky to give up this work; even though she loves it.

One more thing: We are hoping to complete this mission before our father finishes his workout; do you think you could put a rush on this one? We're including the information you need to complete it.

Sincerely;

Kirk, Luke, and Ellen English
Guardians of Grammar Galaxy

Colons & Semicolons
A colon (:) is used to give more information. A semicolon (;) indicates a pause longer than a comma but shorter than a period.

Colons

Use a colon to share an item or list of items. Don't capitalize the items unless they are proper nouns.

Do the right thing: share.
I need the following from the store: French bread, eggs, and milk.

Use a colon between two independent clauses when the second explains the first. The first letter of the clause following the colon is normally capitalized. This is always true when several explanatory sentences or a quote follows.

I have a few rules for you: Clean up after yourself. Brush your teeth. And turn out the lights.
The captain gave this order: "All aboard!"
Capitalizing the first word in lists following a colon is optional unless the list items include complete sentences. In that case, use end marks. Be consistent with capitalization and end marks.

Please pack the following:
– pajamas
– toothbrush
– toothpaste

Things to say to a frustrated student:
– You've been working hard.
– Would you like some help?
– Would it help to take a break?

Semicolons
Use a semicolon to list items that contain commas.

We will be traveling to Lexington, Kentucky; Sioux Falls, South Dakota; and Billings, Montana.
Use a semicolon between two closely related sentences. Unlike sentences with colons, the second sentence is not capitalized.

We are a close family; we spend a lot of time together.
Don't use a semicolon after a dependent clause. Use a comma instead.

After we have dinner, we're going out for ice cream. – correct
Use a semicolon before the words *however*, *therefore*, and *for example* that introduce complete sentences. Follow them with a comma.

I'd like to go on the trip; however, I already have plans.
Use a semicolon before a conjunction connecting independent clauses when the first clause contains a comma.

I think you are smart, talented, and funny; and I'd love to hire you.

☆ <u>Step 1: On Guard & Find the Incorrect Colons and Semicolons</u>
On Guard. *Highlight the correct answer for each of the following questions.*

1. **Highlight the dependent clause in the following sentence:**

   When I finish my side of the closet, I'm going to work on yours.

2. **Highlight the indefinite pronoun in the following sentence:**

   The queen gave several of her dresses to charity.

3. **Highlight the reflexive pronoun in the following sentence:**

   The queen purged her closet herself.

4. **Highlight the demonstrative pronoun in the following sentence:**

   That is why the queen was upset with the king.

5. **Highlight the interrogative pronoun in the following sentence:**

   What happened when the king corrected the queen?

Say each of these words in a sentence. *Examples are given.*

reign – control	My dad couldn't **reign** in the horse he was riding.
supercilious – arrogant	The boy who won the race is **supercilious** about it.
galore – aplenty	Grandpa has hard candy **galore**.

Find the incorrect colons and semicolons. *Read the sentence. Highlight any colons and semicolons that are incorrect.* **Hint:** *The sentence may be correct as written*.

1.   Here's why extra colons are a problem: this newspaper.

2.   After the king went to bed; the queen stayed up to read.

3.   The guidebook gave several punctuation rules; Use a colon to share a list of items. Use a semicolon between closely related sentences. Don't use a semicolon after a dependent clause.

4.   The king wanted to work things out with his wife: however, he also wanted to get to bed.

5.   The queen wanted Kirk, Luke, and Ellen to go to planet Sentence: and she wanted them to go quickly.

6.   Luke brought the following items: his communicator, a book, and a pen.

7.   The queen gave this order; "Come back soon!"

8.   Ellen loved Inky; she felt a connection to her.

⭐ Step 2: Add Colons, Semicolons, and Commas to the Sentences

Add a colon (:), semicolon (;), or comma (,) to each blank below.

1. The king was upset ___ the excess punctuation was irritating.

2. There was one explanation for the excess colons and semicolons ___ Inky.

3. You will need the following for the trip ___ cash, toiletries, change of clothing.

4. When the kids returned ___ the queen hoped the king would be in a better mood.

5. Inky had been a problem before ___ for example ___ she'd added apostrophes where they didn't belong.

6. However ___ Inky was attractive, funny, and popular ___ and she had a loyal following.

7. This is what the queen said before they left ___ "Safe travels!"

8. Inky was a friendly girl ___ she was likely to cooperate.

Activity. *Count how many semicolons and colons you see in a book chapter. Which was most common?*

⭐ Step 3: Rewrite the Sentences Using Correct Punctuation

Write each sentence on the lines below using colons, semicolons, and commas correctly. *You will also need to correct errors in capitalization.*

1. Ellen planned to take the following classes; french cooking, astronomy, and drawing.

_____

_____

_____

2. The queen had three rules about bedtime, brush your teeth. put your clothes away. spend time reading.

_____

_____

_____

3. There are three things never to say to the king. I don't have a book to read. Grammar doesn't matter. Dinner will be late.

_____

_____

_____

4. The kids are learning the history of London, England, Paris, France, and Rome, Italy.

_____

_____

_____

5. The queen thinks the king overreacted, he has high grammar standards.

_____

_____

_____

Vocabulary Victory! Do you remember what these words mean? *Check Step 1 if you need a reminder.*

reign	"We'll talk about it tomorrow," the king said, trying to **reign** in his emotions.
supercilious	"I don't think that's a good idea for you," the queen said in a **supercilious** tone.
galore	Instead, there were colons and semicolons **galore**.

⭐ Advanced Guardians Only

We'd like to offer Inky a free trip to visit you. *Create a packing list of everything she will need for a fun week in your hometown. Put your hometown in the first blank and a colon in the second blank.*

For your trip to _____,
please pack the following ___

☐ _____

☐ _____

☐ _____

☐ _____

☐ _____

☐ _____

☐ _____

☐ _____

☐ _____

☐ _____

☐ _____

☐ _____

Mission 26: Update

Dear guardians,

  Hooray! We aren't using all the colons and semicolons that we were before, thanks to you. You helped us determine which sentences needed them removed. It was a lot of work, but together we got it done.

  Inky was very understanding of the need to stop adding colons and semicolons to every sentence that came to her. Instead of telling her she had to quit completely, we explained that there were specific sentences that needed them. She agreed to follow the rules from the guidebook, so we can let her continue the work that makes her happy. But first, she would like to take a vacation to visit several guardians. She appreciated the packing lists you created.

  We weren't finished with our mission quickly enough to surprise Father after his workout. But he was thrilled to learn that we were working on it. He said to thank you personally.

  We are including the solutions to this mission, so you can be sure we didn't miss an incorrect colon or semicolon.

Sincerely,

Kirk, Luke, and Ellen English

Guardians of Grammar Galaxy

P.S. You finished the Grammar Unit. Congratulations! Please complete the Grammar Challenge that follows. Review Missions 18-26 before you take it.

Step 1 Solutions

On Guard.

1. **Highlight the dependent clause in the following sentence:**

When I finish my side of the closet, I'm going to work on yours.

2. **Highlight the indefinite pronoun in the following sentence:**

The queen gave several of her dresses to charity.

3. **Highlight the reflexive pronoun in the following sentence:**

The queen purged her closet herself.

4. **Highlight the demonstrative pronoun in the following sentence:**

That is why the queen was upset with the king.

5. **Highlight the interrogative pronoun in the following sentence:**

What happened when the king corrected the queen?

Find the incorrect colons and semicolons.

1. Here's why extra colons are a problem: this newspaper.
2. After the king went to bed; the queen stayed up to read.
3. The guidebook gave several punctuation rules; Use a colon to share a list of items. Use a semicolon between closely related sentences. Don't use a semicolon after a dependent clause.
4. The king wanted to work things out with his wife: however, he also wanted to get to bed.
5. The queen wanted Kirk, Luke, and Ellen to go to planet Sentence: and she wanted them to go quickly.
6. Luke brought the following items: his communicator, a book, and a pen.
7. The queen gave this order; "Come back soon!"
8. Ellen loved Inky; she felt a connection to her.

Step 2 Solutions

1. The king was upset; the excess punctuation was irritating.
2. There was one explanation for the excess colons and semicolons: Inky.
3. You will need the following for the trip: cash, toiletries, change of clothing.
4. When the kids returned, the queen hoped the king would be in a better mood.
5. Inky had been a problem before; for example, she'd added apostrophes where they didn't belong.
6. However, Inky was attractive, funny, and popular; and she had a loyal following.
7. This is what the queen said before they left: "Safe travels!"
8. Inky was a friendly girl; she was likely to cooperate.

Step 3 Solutions

1. Ellen planned to take the following classes: **French** cooking, astronomy, and drawing.
2. The queen had three rules about bedtime: **Brush** your teeth. **Put** your clothes away. **Spend** time reading.
3. There are three things never to say to the king: I don't have a book to read. Grammar doesn't matter. Dinner will be late.
4. The kids are learning the history of London, England; Paris, France; and Rome, Italy.
5. The queen thinks the king overreacted; he has high grammar standards.

Grammar Challenge 1

*Carefully read all the possible answers and then highlight the letter for the **one** best answer.*

1. **A colon (:) is used to give more:**
   a. information
   b. pause than a semicolon
   c. cookies

2. **Don't use a semicolon:**
   a. between two closely related independent clauses
   b. to list items that contain commas
   c. after a dependent clause

3. **After we had dinner, we went to a movie.**
   Which of the following is true of the sentence above?
   a. *After we had dinner* is a dependent clause.
   b. The sentence is a complex sentence.
   c. both a and b

4. **Any player who breaks the rules will be eliminated.**
   In this sentence, <u>any</u> is:
   a. an indefinite adjective
   b. in agreement with a singular verb
   c. both a and b

5. **I gave myself a haircut.**
   In this sentence, <u>myself</u> is:
   a. a direct object
   b. a reflexive pronoun
   c. neither a nor b

6. **This is my daughter.**
   In this sentence, <u>this</u> is:
   a. a demonstrative pronoun
   b. a demonstrative adjective
   c. a reflexive pronoun

7. **Whatever did you think you were doing?**

   In this sentence, which word is the interrogative pronoun?

   a. did

   b. whatever

   c. doing

8. **Me and Caleb are going to the store.**

   What is the correct version of the above sentence?

   a. *Caleb and I are going to the store.*

   b. Caleb and me are going to the store.

   c. Me and Caleb are going to the store.

9. **I love to sleep in a big, comfy bed.**

   In this sentence, <u>bed</u> is:

   a. the participle

   b. object of the preposition

   c. dependent clause

10. **I ran into the closed door.**

   In the sentence, <u>closed</u> is:

   a. a participle

   b. an adjective

   c. both a and b

Number Correct:_____/10

☆ *Advanced Guardian Vocabulary Challenge*
For an extra challenge, highlight the word that belongs in each blank.

1. **The boy who won the race is _____ about it.**
   reign   supercilious   exasperated

2. **I was _____ when the faucet kept dripping all night.**
   peeved   galore   altercation

3. **My grandma tries to save plants, but they usually _____.**
   streamline   purged   deteriorate

4. **My friend _____ me for not getting sick on the roller coaster.**
   errant   commended   tremulously

5. **The monkey at the zoo held onto its banana _____.**
   resolutely   proactive   discern

6. **My parents don't like _____.**
   encounter   donned   bickering

7. **The dolphins _____ the ship.**
   neglecting   trailed   unrest

8. **I was pretty _____ about not getting a pet snake for my birthday.**
   morose   reverie   mimicking

9. **The rude cashier answered me _____.**
   aerial   contained   tersely

Number Correct:_____/9

Grammar Challenge 1 Answers
1.a; 2.c; 3.c; 4.c; 5.b; 6.a; 7.b; 8.a; 9.b; 10.c

If you got 9 or more correct, congratulations! You've earned your Grammar star. You may add it to your Grammar Guardian bookmark. You are ready for an adventure in composition and speaking.

If you did not get 9 or more correct, don't worry. You have another chance. You may want to review the information from each chapter you've read so far. Then take the Grammar Challenge 2. Remember to **choose the <u>one</u> best answer**.

Advanced Guardian Vocabulary Challenge Answers
1. supercilious
2. peeved
3. deteriorate
4. commended
5. resolutely
6. bickering
7. trailed
8. morose
9. tersely

Grammar Challenge 2

Carefully read all the possible answers and then *highlight the letter for the* **one** *best answer.*

1. **Do the right thing share.**
   Which is the correct version of the sentence above?
   a. Do the right thing: share.
   b. Do the right thing, share.
   c. Do the right thing share.

2. **I'd like to go on the trip; however I already have plans.**
   Which is the correct version of the sentence above?
   a. I'd like to go on the trip, however I already have plans.
   b. I'd like to go on the trip; however, I already have plans.
   c. I'd like to go on the trip; however I already have plans.

3. **The words after, before, and when are:**
   a. common subordinating conjunctions
   b. common objects of the preposition
   c. neither a nor b

4. **The words someone, neither, and several are:**
   a. definite pronouns
   b. indefinite pronouns
   c. neither a nor b

5. **The words myself, ourselves, and itself are:**
   a. dependent pronouns
   b. indefinite pronouns
   c. reflexive pronouns

6. **The words this, that, these, and those are:**
   a. demonstrative pronounous
   b. demonstrative adjectives
   c. either a or b

7. The word <u>whom</u> is:
   a. an interrogative pronoun
   b. a subjective pronoun
   c. neither a nor b

8. The word <u>her</u> is:
   a. a semicolon
   b. an objective pronoun
   c. a participle

9. An object of the preposition is a:
   a. noun
   b. pronoun
   c. either a or b

10. Which of the following words is a present participle or gerund?
   a. listened
   b. listening
   c. listens

Number Correct:_____/10

Grammar Challenge 2 Answers
1.a; 2.b; 3.a; 4.b; 5.c; 6.c; 7.a; 8.b; 9.c; 10.b

If you got 9 or more correct, congratulations! You've earned your Grammar star. You may add a star to your bookmark. You are now ready for an adventure in composition and speaking.

If you did not get 9 or more correct, don't worry. Review the questions you missed. You may want to get more practice using the resources at GrammarGalaxyBooks.com/RedStar for grammar. Your teacher can ask you other questions like the ones you missed and if you get them correct, you'll have earned your Grammar star and can move on to an adventure in composition and speaking.

Unit IV: Adventures in Composition & Speaking

Mission 27: Business Letter

GrammarGalaxyKids.com
1 Castle Way
Planet English 12345

January 10, 3000

To whom it may concern:

We are practicing writing a business letter, even though you're our friends. As you may have heard, Movie Adventureland is now open. We are so excited to go to this new resort, but the ticket prices are high. Father doesn't want to spend the money right now.

But our father did have a great idea. He suggested writing the resort and requesting tickets in exchange for a resort review on our new website. The only trouble is, we didn't know how to write a good business letter until now.

Your mission from us has two purposes. First, we want you to learn how to write business letters too. And second, we are hoping you will write a letter to Movie Adventureland as well, explaining that you want to read our review. More potential readers may convince the resort to give us free tickets.

We hope you are willing to help us, and we look forward to receiving your completed mission soon. See the information we're including to help you.

Sincerely,

Kirk, Luke, and Ellen English

Guardians of Grammar Galaxy
grammargalaxybooks@gmail.com

Business Letters

Business letters are often written to create a professional **impression** and/or to persuade. The audience for a business letter is typically someone you don't know. Follow a specific format when writing a business letter.

Business letters should be typed on plain or letterhead paper. Letterhead paper already has your name or your company name and address printed on it. When using plain paper, put this information at the top of the letter.

Insert a line space and add today's date.

Then address the individual you want to read your letter. This should be a specific person. Do some research or call the business to determine who is in charge of the department you are writing to. Start the salutation with *Dear Mr.* or *Ms. Last Name* and end with a colon (:). When you don't have a name, you will have to write *To whom it may concern:*.

Add a line space after the salutation.

Then begin and continue your letter with no idents. Paragraphs are separated by line spaces. This is called block format. Your letter should have one-inch margins. You can set these in the word processing program you are using.

Be sure to provide all the information the person needs to understand who you are and what you want. Be polite and give your recipient reason to respond positively to your request. This is the most important part of a business letter.

Add a line space and then the closing followed by a comma. An appropriate closing for a business letter is *Sincerely* or *Cordially*.

Add two line spaces where you will put your written signature after printing the letter.

Then add your full name followed by your title (if any).

Finally, add contact information, such as your phone number, if it is not included in your letterhead.

Proofread your letter twice and ask someone else to proofread it for you too.

⭐ Step 1: On Guard & Identify Correct Business Letter Format

On Guard. *Highlight the correct answer for each question.*

1. Use a _____ before the words <u>however</u> and <u>therefore</u>.

   colon   semicolon   comma

2. Dependent clauses with a subordinating conjunction at the beginning of a sentence are normally followed by a _____.

   colon   semicolon   comma

3. Indefinite pronouns ending in -one, -body, and -thing are always:

   singular   plural   subjective

4. Reflexive pronouns <u>cannot</u> serve as:

   subjects   objects   indirect objects

5. This, that, these, and those are demonstrative adjectives when they are followed by:

   verbs   nouns   contractions

Say each of these words in a sentence. *Examples are given.*

exorbitant – excessive	The price of soda at the theater is **exorbitant**.
ruffled – messed	My dog **ruffled** my newly made bed.
impression – reaction	The clown did not make a positive **impression** on my baby sister.

Identify correct business letter format. *Review our letter to Movie Adventureland resort. Highlight YES or NO for each question about its formatting.*

Dear Movie Adventureland Resort,

How are you? We are doing well.

We saw that you opened your resort, and it looks amazing. We really want to see the Jumanji and Jurassic Park attractions. However, your ticket prices are way too high and our father won't let us buy them.

So we have an idea. Will you let us come to the resort for free if we write a review for you? We would put the review on our new website. Please give us your answer right away. We're excited!

Sincerely,

Kirk, Luke, and Ellen English

---

1. Is the letter typed?	YES	NO
2. Is the letter on letterhead paper, or does it include a name and address at the top of the letter?	YES	NO
3. Does the letter include the date?	YES	NO
4. Does the letter mention a specific person or To whom it may concern followed by a colon?	YES	NO
5. Is the letter written in block format?	YES	NO
6. Does the letter provide all the information needed to understand who you are and what you want?	YES	NO
7. Does the letter include a closing of Sincerely or Cordially followed by a comma?	YES	NO
8. Is other contact information included at the end of the letter?	YES	NO

⭐ Review Our Revised Business Letter

We've made some changes to our letter to Movie Adventureland.

Highlight YES or NO for the questions about our format again.

April 1, 3000

Dear Ms. de Vil:

Congratulations on the opening of Movieland Adventure Resort! It looks exciting from the few pictures we have seen. We know that you want as many people to visit your resort as possible.

We have a proposal for you. In exchange for complimentary tickets, we would publish a review of your resort on our new website GrammarGalaxyKids.com. We regularly communicate with thousands of grammar guardians who would read and share our review. Many of them will visit the resort as a result.

We would be happy to discuss the details with you at your convenience.

Sincerely,

Kirk, Luke, and Ellen English

---

1. Is the letter typed?	YES	NO
2. Is the letter on letterhead paper, or does it include a name and address at the top of the letter?	YES	NO
3. Does the letter include the date?	YES	NO
4. Does the letter mention a specific person or To whom it may concern followed by a colon?	YES	NO
5. Is the letter written in block format?	YES	NO
6. Does the letter provide all the information needed to understand who you are and what you want?	YES	NO
7. Does the letter include a closing of Sincerely or Cordially followed by a comma?	YES	NO
8. Is other contact information included at the end of the letter?	YES	NO

Activity. *Ask an adult family member for a business letter they've received from a company trying to earn your family's business. What did the letter writer do well? What could be improved?*

⭐ Step 3: Draft a Business Letter to Movie Adventureland

Use the form below to write a first draft of a business letter to convince the resort to allow us to write a review. *Remember that it has to be in the resort's best interest for them to agree.*

<<<Name and Address

<<<Date

Dear Ms. de Vil:

Sincerely,

<<<Signature

<<<Phone or email

GrammarGalaxyBooks.com
grammargalaxybooks@gmail.com

Vocabulary Victory! Do you remember what these words mean? *Check Step 1 if you need a reminder.*

exorbitant	The ticket prices are **exorbitant**.
ruffled	The king smiled and **ruffled** Luke's hair.
impression	Business letters are often written to create a professional **impression**.

☆ Advanced Guardians Only

Type the letter you wrote in Step 3. *Print it, proofread it twice, and ask your teacher to proofread it. Make any needed changes. Get your teacher's help with the following: Print a copy of Grammar Guardian letterhead from GrammarGalaxyBooks.com/RedStar. Put your printed letter on top of the letterhead, so you can see the color through the paper with your letter on it. Does it fit? If not, add line spaces or change the font or margins. Make changes until the letter will fit nicely on the letterhead. Then feed the letterhead through your printer so that your letter prints on the colored side of the letterhead. If you don't know which way to put the paper into the feed, consult your printer manual or use a test paper with writing on it.*

Mission 27: Update

GrammarGalaxyKids.com
1 Castle Way
Planet English 12345

January 14, 3000

Dear Mr. and Ms. Guardian:

We are still practicing our business writing, so that's why we're using this letter format. We can't wait to give you the good news: We will get free tickets for our review of Movie Adventureland! That's in large part thanks to your letters. The marketing director at Movie Adventureland was so impressed with your writing. Thank you! We will let you know when our review is finished.

Now that you know how to write a business letter, you may be able to arrange a discount or free gift from the businesses you write to. Good writing skills can be profitable!

We are including the solutions to your mission.

Sincerely,

Kirk, Luke, and Ellen English

Guardians of Grammar Galaxy
grammargalaxybooks@gmail.com

Step 1 Solutions

On Guard.

1. Use a _____ before the words <u>however</u> and <u>therefore</u>.
   colon   semicolon   comma

2. Dependent clauses with a subordinating conjunction at the beginning of a sentence are normally followed by a
   _____.
   colon   semicolon   comma

3. Indefinite pronouns ending in -one, -body, and -thing are always:
   singular   plural   subjective

4. Reflexive pronouns <u>cannot</u> serve as:
   subjects   objects   indirect objects

5. This, that, these, and those are demonstrative adjectives when they are followed by:
   verbs   nouns   contractions

Identify correct business letter format.

	YES	NO
1. Is the letter typed?	YES	NO
2. Is the letter on letterhead paper, or does it include a name and address at the top of the letter?	YES	NO
3. Does the letter include the date?	YES	NO
4. Does the letter mention a specific person or To whom it may concern followed by a colon?	YES	NO
5. Is the letter written in block format?	YES	NO
6. Does the letter provide all the information needed to understand who you are and what you want?	YES	NO
7. Does the letter include a closing of Sincerely or Cordially followed by a comma?	YES	NO
8. Is other contact information included at the end of the letter?	YES	NO

Step 2 Solutions

	YES	NO
1. Is the letter typed?	YES	NO
2. Is the letter on letterhead paper, or does it include a name and address at the top of the letter?	YES	NO
3. Does the letter include the date?	YES	NO
4. Does the letter mention a specific person or To whom it may concern followed by a colon?	YES	NO
5. Is the letter written in block format?	YES	NO
6. Does the letter provide all the information needed to understand who you are and what you want?	YES	NO
7. Does the letter include a closing of Sincerely or Cordially followed by a comma?	YES	NO
8. Is other contact information included at the end of the letter?	YES	NO

Mission 28: Descriptive Writing

Dear guardians,

We scheduled a date to visit Movie Adventureland, and we're excited to go. But our father taught us a very important writing skill we need before we write our review: descriptive writing.

If we just give the facts about the park, no one will want to buy tickets. The Movie Adventureland marketing department will be disappointed in our review. It's descriptive language that forms pictures in the mind and gets kids excited about theme parks, food, and even books.

Father says every guardian should know how to write using sensory language. That's what this mission is all about. Describe the places you have visited with descriptive writing, and who knows? Maybe we'll plan a visit ourselves.

Sincerely,

Kirk, Luke, and Ellen English

Guardians of Grammar Galaxy

P.S. We're including information about descriptive writing on the next page.

Descriptive Writing

Descriptive writing uses words to describe subjects so that a picture is formed in a reader's mind. Word pictures are created with sensory words, analogies (similes and metaphors), or both.

<u>Sensory Words</u>

Sensory words are strong vocabulary words related to sight, sound, smell, taste, and touch. Before writing a descriptive first draft, make a list of sensory words that describe your subject. Sensory words that could describe cotton candy include:

  – sight (turquoise, hot pink, whipped, airy, fluffy)
  – sound (grinding motor of the machine, shrill call of the salesperson, pleading children's requests)
  – smell (fruity, sweet)
  – taste (sugary, tangy)
  – touch (sticky, gritty, smooth cone)

<u>Analogies</u>

Before writing your descriptive first draft, consider what your subject is like, using a simile or metaphor.

The cotton candy was like a cloud in my hand. (simile)

The cotton candy was a truffula tree that I chopped down eagerly. (metaphor)

<u>Organize Your Description</u>

Once you have ideas for descriptive language ready, decide if you will organize your description chronologically (by time), by importance, or by location.

  – Buying the cotton candy, eating it, and cleaning up after it (chronological)
  – Being excited to eat the candy, only to discover it is too sweet (importance)
  – Seeing the cotton candy in a machine outside a stadium and later eating it in the stands (location)

Refer to your sensory words and analogies as you write your description chronologically, by importance, or by location.

☆ Step 1: On Guard & Choose Sensory Words

On Guard. *Highlight the correct answer for each question.*

1. The salutation of a business letter ends with a:
   comma   colon   period

2. When the first independent clause contains commas, follow it with a:
   comma   semicolon   question mark

3. A sentence containing a dependent and independent clause is:
   complex   simple   interrogative

4. <u>Each</u>, <u>either</u>, and <u>neither</u> are:
   singular   plural   demonstrative

5. Reflexive pronouns may also be used as _____ pronouns.
   subjective   demonstrative   intensive

Say each of these words in a sentence. *Examples are given.*

pristine – perfect	My room doesn't have to be **pristine**, just picked up.
demurely – modestly	Mother says we should accept compliments **demurely**.
protocol – etiquette	Picking your nose in public isn't proper **protocol**.

Choose sensory words. *Choose one place you've visited to describe. Then highlight any of the sensory words listed below that describe your location. Finally, add your own descriptive words for the location.*

Sight

blue skies	bustling crowds	turquoise water
bright red sunburn	mossy trees	neon lights
circling birds	cobblestone streets	neat rows of bleachers

_____   _____   _____

_____   _____   _____

_____   _____   _____

Sound

flag flapping	chatter	waves crashing
seagulls crying	leaves rustling	merchants calling
crows cawing	heels clicking	crowd cheering

_____   _____   _____

_____   _____   _____

_____   _____   _____

Smell

buttered popcorn	pungent coffee	musty seaweed
earthy rain	pine	charcoal grill
suntan lotion	exhaust fumes	sweet cotton candy

_____   _____   _____

_____   _____   _____

_____   _____   _____

Taste

salty popcorn	bitter coffee	salty air
tart lemonade	savory sausage	biting mustard
refreshing water	spicy sauce	greasy burger

_____   _____   _____

_____   _____   _____

_____   _____   _____

<u>Touch</u>

rough fence post	smooth glass	sticky pavement
gritty sand	slippery rocks	humid air
chilly water	leathery chairs	hot bleachers

_____   _____   _____

_____   _____   _____

_____   _____   _____

⭐ Step 2: Choose an Analogy and Way of Organizing Your Description

Choose a metaphor/simile that describes the place you've visited. *Highlight one of the analogies below or write your own by answering the question.* **Note:** *Your choice should be metaphorical and not actual. If you visited a cave, don't choose cave.*

rainbow	frying pan	heaven
cave	story book	castle
igloo	desert	ghost town
eye of the storm	zoo	toy store

What does the place you visited remind you of?

_____

Highlight how you will organize your description. *Then write the three main parts of the location you will describe.*

chronologically   importance   location

1._____

2._____

3._____

Activity. *Draw a color picture of this object based on the description below. What do you think it is?*

Against a cold and tar-black backdrop dotted with thousands of white drops of light hangs a buttery yellow orb. It is streaked with warm shades of cream, brown, and green as though it has been spun on a potter's wheel. While it appears to be solid, the striped sphere's outer layer is gas. The ball of gas is surrounded by a racetrack of colorful lanes. Ice, rock, and dust travel in the lanes, creating the appearance of white, gray, and black rings.

⭐ Step 3: Write Your Description

Using the preparation from Steps 1 and 2, write a first draft of your description on the next page. *Use this formula:*

(Place) is (analogy).

Walt Disney World is like a storybook.

How organized.

The resort is a fairy tale from start to finish. (chronological)

My favorite memories of the visit are... (importance)

Each park in Walt Disney World is unique. (location)

Use sight, sound, taste, smell, and touch words in your description.

Booming explosions of fireworks drowned out the crowd noise.

The cool mist from the fans seemed to sizzle on my burning skin.

Conclude with a review and another analogy reference.

After visiting three of Walt Disney World's parks, I felt like I'd finished a book that I'm looking forward to reading again soon.

Review

Read your description out loud. Could it use more sensory words to help the reader form a picture? Did you use transition words to help the reader know when you're describing another part (first, next, also)? Correct any punctuation, spelling, or grammar errors you find.

Vocabulary Victory! Do you remember what these words mean? *Check Step 1 if you need a reminder.*

pristine	I asked the gardener to make sure everything is **pristine**.
demurely	"Oh, thank you," the queen said **demurely**.
protocol	The photographer agreed and bowed awkwardly, uncertain of **protocol**.

☆ <u>Advanced Guardians Only</u>

Create a travel flyer. *Type your written description and add pictures your family took or pictures you find online with your teacher's help. Have your teacher proofread your flyer. You may want to print the completed flyer on glossy paper.*

Mission 28: Update

Dear guardians,

   We received your descriptions of places you've visited, and now we have a huge list of places we want to go! Thanks so much for those.

   We did visit Movie Adventureland, but we aren't going to write you about it quite yet. We'll just say it was a blast!

   We are including the solutions to this mission. Keep writing descriptively to keep the galaxy strong.

Sincerely,

Kirk, Luke, and Ellen English

Guardians of Grammar Galaxy

Step 1 Solutions

On Guard.

1. The salutation of a business letter ends with a:
   comma   colon   period

2. When the first independent clause contains commas, follow it with a:
   comma   semicolon   question mark

3. A sentence containing a dependent and independent clause is:
   complex   simple   interrogative

4. Each, either, and neither are:
   singular   plural   demonstrative

5. Reflexive pronouns may also be used as _____ pronouns.
   subjective   demonstrative   intensive

Activity. You should have drawn a planet resembling Saturn.

Mission 29: Sentence Starters

Dear guardians,

      The reason for this mission is the Sentence Relays on planet Sentence. The word *the* was chosen to be lead runner for all sentences because of its experience. The problem with this is that beginning every sentence with the word *the* is very repetitive in speaking and writing. The review of Movie Adventureland we started is written this way.

      The plan now is to change the running order for the Sentence Relays. The way to make the plan work is to have you help us choose new sentence starters like adverbs, participles, prepositional phrases, two adjectives, transitions, and subordinating conjunctions. The information you need is below. The hope we now have is in you!

Sincerely,

Kirk, Luke, and Ellen English
The Guardians of Grammar Galaxy

Sentence Starters

There are a number of ways to begin a sentence to keep your readers' interest. Rather than beginning with an article adjective (a, an, the) or the subject of the sentence, try beginning your sentence with:
- **an adverb** *Slowly* the man backed away from the bear.
- **a prepositional phrase** *At the start of the game*, the kids got along well.
- **a participle** *Gasping* for breath, the swimmer emerged from the water.
- **two adjectives** *Cold and hungry*, the skier entered the warm cabin.
- **transition words** *Third*, let the paint dry for eight hours.
- **subordinating conjunctions** *Whether* it rains or not, we are having the picnic. These sentence starters will keep your writing from sounding repetitive.

⭐ <u>Step 1: On Guard & Identify the Type of Sentence Starter</u>
On Guard. *Highlight the correct answer for each question.*

1. Descriptive writing uses which type of words?
   overused   pronouns   sensory

2. The closing of a business letter should be:
   Cheers,   Sincerely,   Love,

3. The punctuation mark that should follow <u>Please pack the following</u>
   :   ;   ,

4. The word <u>while</u> is what type of conjunction?
   coordinating   subordinating   dependent

5. Which word belongs in the blank? Most of the kids _____ Grammar Galaxy.
   likes   love   enjoys

Say each of these words in a sentence. *Examples are given.*

postpone – delay	My tooth hurts so much that I can't **postpone** going to the dentist.
conciliatory – peacemaking	I accidentally hit my friend and began speaking in a **conciliatory** way.
interminable – endless	The wait before summer vacation seems **interminable**.

Identify the type of sentence starter. Read the sentence. *Highlight the type of sentence starter it uses.* **Note:** <u>*Conjunction refers to subordinating conjunction*</u>.

1. **The king thought something was wrong with the kids' review.**
   article   participle   adverb

2. **Ellen wasn't happy about interrupting their game.**
   article   preposition   subject

3. **Thoughtfully the king read their resort review.**
   preposition   adverb   participle

4. **When he had trouble requesting the guidebook, the king went to the library himself.**
   conjunction   participle   two adjectives

5. **In the library, the king read the guidebook.**
   conjunction   preposition   two adjectives

6. **Reading the article helped the English family understand.**
   participle   adverb   preposition

7. **Calm and agreeable, the kids agree to rewrite the review.**
   adverb   two adjectives   preposition

8. **First, the kids packed snacks for their trip.**
   transition words   two adjectives   participle

☆ Step 2: Rewrite Sentences Using Sentence Starters

Using the sentence starter in parentheses, rewrite the sentences on the lines.

1. The kids eagerly agreed to go to planet Sentence. (adverb)

_____

_____

2. The review article, repetitive and boring, needs revision. (two adjectives)

_____

_____

3. The children would need the guardians' help before their trip. (preposition)

_____

_____

4. The king began closing the book and helped write the mission. (participle)

_____

_____

5. The sentences will all begin with an article if the guardians don't help. (subordinating conjunction)

_____

_____

Activity. *See how long you can go starting <u>every</u> sentence you say with the word* **the**.

☆ Step 3: Rewrite Sentences Using Unique Sentence Starters

Rewrite the sentences using each type of sentence starter.
Highlight each sentence starter below when you've used it. **Hint:** *Change some words in rewriting the sentences.*

adverb	prepositional phrase	participle
2 adjectives	transition words	subordinating conjunction

1. The queen gave the kids snacks when she heard about their trip.

_____

_____

2. The warm cookies she packed carefully.

_____

_____

3. The baking of cookies was a new hobby for the queen.

_____

_____

4. The gooey and sweet cookies would be a hit with the children.

_____

_____

5. The note of encouragement she put by the snacks.

_____

_____

6. The next step she took was to pack drinks.

_____

_____

Vocabulary Victory! Do you remember what these words mean? *Check Step 1 if you need a reminder.*

postpone	You shouldn't **postpone** it.
conciliatory	"I will ask Screen to pull it up for us," Kirk said to be **conciliatory**.
interminable	The sign advertising the **interminable** wait time did not seem to put these families off.

☆ <u>Advanced Guardians Only</u>

Rewrite your location description using new sentence starters.
Change some of the sentence starters in your description from Mission 28 to include the new starters you've learned. You may write on the lines below or make the changes to your typed document.

_____

_____

_____

_____

_____

_____

_____

_____

_____

_____

_____

_____

_____

_____

_____

_____

_____

_____

_____

_____

_____

Mission 29: Update

Dear friends,

     Slowly we were able to get the running order for the Sentence Relays changed. In a crisis, we can count on you! Writing with different sentence starters, as you did, made things easier for us on planet Sentence. Tired but happy, we are back home and ready to change some of the sentences beginning with *the* in our resort review.

     Though we probably don't need to remind you, please check your mission solutions with the answers we are sending you. Finally, did you notice that we started every sentence of this update letter with a different sentence starter?

Sincerely,

Kirk, Luke, and Ellen English
Guardians of Grammar Galaxy

Step 1 Solutions

On Guard.

1. Descriptive writing uses which type of words?
   overused   pronouns   sensory

2. The closing of a business letter should be:
   Cheers,   Sincerely,   Love,

3. The punctuation mark that should follow Please pack the following
   :   ;   ,

4. The word while is what type of conjunction?
   coordinating   subordinating   dependent

5. Which word belongs in the blank? Most of the kids _____ Grammar Galaxy.
   likes   love   enjoys

Identify the type of sentence starter.

1. **The king thought something was wrong with the kids' review.**
   article   participle   adverb

2. **Ellen wasn't happy about interrupting their game.**
   article   preposition   subject

3. **Thoughtfully the king read their resort review.**
   preposition   adverb   participle

4. **When he had trouble requesting the guidebook, the king went to the library himself.**
   conjunction   participle   two adjectives

5. **In the library, the king read the guidebook.**
   conjunction   preposition   two adjectives

6. **Reading the article helped the English family understand.**
   participle   adverb   preposition

7. **Calm and agreeable, the kids agree to rewrite the review.**
   adverb   two adjectives   preposition

8. **First, the kids packed snacks for their trip.**
   transition words   two adjectives   participle

Step 2 Solutions – answers may vary

1. Eagerly the kids agreed to go to planet Sentence. (adverb)
2. Repetitive and boring, the review article needs revision. (two adjectives)
3. Before their trip, the children would need the guardians' help. (preposition)
4. Closing the book, the king helped write the mission. (participle)
5. if the guardians don't help, the sentences will all begin with an article. (subordinating conjunction)

Step 3 Solutions – answers may vary

adverb   prepositional phrase   participle
2 adjectives   transition words   subordinating conjunction

1. When she heard about their trip, the queen gave the kids snacks.
2. Carefully she packed the warm cookies.
3. Baking cookies was a new hobby for the queen.
4. Gooey and sweet, the cookies would be a hit with the children.
5. By the snacks, she put a note of encouragement.
6. Next, she packed drinks.

Mission 30: Writing with a Partner

Dear guardians,

We are writing the review of Movie Adventureland together, and our father pointed out a problem with it. Luke finished his part of the review at the last minute (as usual). Now the whole thing sounds like it's been copied and pasted together, which it has. This is Ellen, by the way.

We thought we had the review done well. It includes a lot of descriptive writing and numerous, unique sentence starters. But we each write in a different style. I like accurate writing and Ellen's is a bit more emotional, I would say? This is Kirk.

My part of the review was great! Really, Kirk's part was too boring, and Ellen's was too girly. So now we have to rewrite it because they don't write as well as I do! Ha ha. I'm going to let Ellen do the final writing because she'll be mad otherwise. This is Luke.

I hope you don't believe what Luke just wrote. This is Ellen again. What these two dear brothers of mine didn't say is that we all need to learn how to write well with a partner. It can be challenging but fun. Complete this mission and work with another guardian, a sibling, or a friend. We know you can do it!

Find the information you need on the next page.

Sincerely,

Kirk, Luke, and Ellen English

Guardians of Grammar Galaxy

Writing with a Partner

Writing with a partner can improve your writing and be fun. But writing with a partner can also produce conflict.

To have a good writing partnership:

-Agree on a meeting schedule. Decide on times to meet and what must be accomplished between meetings. If possible, meet in person. Otherwise, decide how you will discuss your writing project.

-Write separately, without concern for what your writing partner will think. Edit your work so it is ready for your partner to review at your next meeting.

-Edit together. Have each writer read his or her own work while the partner actively listens. After listening, the partner should respond with positive comments such as "I noticed," "I felt," or "I pictured."

To help the writer improve, the partner should make statements that begin with "Say more about..." or "Can you explain...?" Make changes together as a result of these discussions.

-Write with one voice. Work written by more than one person may have multiple styles or voices. To give your work a unified style, have one partner go through the piece and add personal touches.

-Do a final edit. Read through the work together after one partner has written the piece in one voice. Make any spelling, punctuation, or grammar changes needed.

⭐ Step 1: On Guard & Arrange to Write with a Partner

On Guard. *Highlight TRUE or FALSE for each statement.*

1. Two adjectives make a good sentence starter.   TRUE   FALSE

2. Descriptive writing may use analogies.   TRUE   FALSE

3. Business letter paragraphs should be indented.   TRUE   FALSE

4. Be consistent with capitalization and end marks   TRUE   FALSE
   in lists following a colon.

5. Awesome is a subordinating conjunction.   TRUE   FALSE

Say each of these words in a sentence. *Examples are given.*

lofted – launched	I **lofted** a paper airplane that hit my dad in the nose.
negotiate – discuss	I plan to **negotiate** for a higher allowance.
defiantly – rebelliously	I brush my hair, but some of it still sticks out **defiantly**.

Arrange to write with a partner. *Visit a new place with a friend, sibling, or other family member. While at the location, decide together if you will organize your review chronologically, by importance, or by location. Choose an analogy for your location and your review's three main parts. Decide who will write the introduction and first part of the review and who will write the second and third part of the review. Finally, choose a date and time to review your writing with your partner.* **Note:** <u>The conclusion will be written last.</u>

Place_____

Visit date and time_____

Highlight whether the review is:
- chronological
- by importance
- by location

Place is like_____

<u>Three main parts of review:</u>
1._____
2._____
3._____

Introduction / first part writer_____

Second / third part writer_____

Writing review date and time_____

☆ Step 2: Write Your Section of the Review

Write your section of the review without concern for your partner's opinion. *Use the sensory word prompts to help you write descriptively about the place you visited. Use the lines on the following page to write a draft of your section of the review or type it.*

Sight

_____ _____ _____
_____ _____ _____

Sound

_____ _____ _____
_____ _____ _____

Smell

_____ _____ _____
_____ _____ _____

Taste

_____ _____ _____
_____ _____ _____

Touch

_____ _____ _____
_____ _____ _____

Activity. *Make a recipe with a partner. Your partner should make the first half and you should work on the second half. Would making the recipe be easier or harder if you did it yourself? Is there a better way to share the work?*

⭐ <u>Step 3: Meet with Your Partner to Review Writing</u>
Take turns reading what you've written with a partner.
Use the prompts below to comment on the writing. Then make changes to what you've each written as a result of the discussion. Finally, write a conclusion for your review together. Remember that the conclusion is a short review of what you've said, including another mention of the analogy you chose.

I noticed...
I felt...
I pictured...
Say more about...
Can you explain...?

Conclusion:

_____
_____
_____
_____
_____
_____

Vocabulary Victory! Do you remember what these words mean?
Check Step 1 if you need a reminder.

lofted	The king ran for it and was able to just hit it so that it was **lofted** high over the net.
negotiate	Kirk tried to **negotiate** peace.
defiantly	"Maybe," he said **defiantly**.

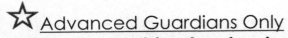 ☆ <u>Advanced Guardians Only</u>

Write your combined review in your voice. *As you use your own style in editing the review, be sure to add transition words (e.g., first, next) between the parts of the review. Type the combined review. Schedule a time with your partner to do a final edit. Make any spelling, punctuation, or grammar changes needed.*

Day and time to edit_____

Mission 30: Update

Dear guardian friends,

We are so happy to report that our review of Movie Adventureland is finished! We edited the review, Ellen put it in her voice, and it's been proofread. It will be up on the Grammar Galaxy Kids website soon. Whew! It was quite a bit of work, but we think you'll enjoy reading it.

What did you think of writing with a partner? Do you prefer to write alone or together? Either way, learning to write with someone else is a good skill to have.

We are including the solutions to the On Guard section for you to check.

Sincerely,

Kirk, Luke, and Ellen English

Guardians of Grammar Galaxy

Step 1 Solutions

On Guard.

1.	Two adjectives make a good sentence starter.	TRUE	FALSE
2.	Descriptive writing may use analogies.	TRUE	FALSE
3.	Business letter paragraphs should be indented.	TRUE	FALSE
4.	Be consistent with capitalization and end marks in lists following a colon.	TRUE	FALSE
5.	<u>Awesome</u> is a subordinating conjunction.	TRUE	FALSE

Mission 31: Creating Titles

Dear friends and fellow guardians,

We know you haven't yet read our review of Movie Adventureland because our website shows no views. We thought the Gremlin was blocking access to our site, but now we know it's because our title wasn't interesting enough.

We are going to create a list of new titles that include words people are searching online. But we need your help choosing the best title. We also need you to learn how to create titles for your own writing. We've learned how important that is! Please complete this mission so that your hard work in writing will get people reading.

We're including information about titles from *The Guidebook to Grammar Galaxy* to help you.

Sincerely,

Kirk, Luke, and Ellen English
Guardians of Grammar Galaxy

Creating Titles

A good title has three characteristics: 1) interests readers, 2) communicates content, and 3) shares the author's attitude toward the subject.

Creating the best title requires brainstorming. Respond to these 10 title prompts. Narrow your choice to your top three. Then ask others for their favorite.

1. Write a title that's a question.
2. Use a sensory image from your writing as a title.
3. Write a title beginning with an -ing verb.
4. Write a one- or two-word title.
5. Write a three-word title.
6. Write a four-word title.
7. Write a five-word title.
8. Use a common saying or quote as a title.
9. Change one word in the title from #8.
10. Put two of these titles together with a colon [:].*

*Inspired by the University of Minnesota's Writing Center's adaptation of Richard Leahy's "Twenty Titles for the Writer." http://writing.umn.edu/sws/assets/pdf/quicktips/titles.pdf

☆ Step 1: On Guard & Search Review Titles

On Guard. *Answer the questions or answer them verbally for your teacher.*

1. Name one way of successfully writing with a partner.

2. Name one type of sentence starter.

3. What are the five senses used in descriptive writing?

4. What is one way of organizing your descriptive writing?

5. What is the most important part of a business letter?

Say each of these words in a sentence. *Examples are given.*

earnestly– seriously	I **earnestly** intended to clean my room.
compelling – irresistible	The warm cookies were just too **compelling** for me.
negligence – failure	The crayons went through the wash because of my **negligence**.

Search review titles. *With your teacher's help, do an internet search for reviews of a place you haven't visited but might like to. Write three titles that appear in the search results that are compelling (i.e., reviews you'd like to read). You may have to look through a few pages of results to find them.* **Note**: *The title should not be simply (Place) Review.*

_____

_____

_____

_____

_____

☆ <u>Step 2: Do SEO Research for One of the Places You've Described</u>

With your teacher's help, put both of the places you've written about in previous missions into a search engine. *Type in "(Place Name) review". The search engine will make automatic suggestions as you type. These are the keywords people are searching for. What are they? Write them below.*

_____

_____

_____

_____

_____

_____

_____

_____

Activity. *Which of these review titles for Ferrari Land in Spain interests you most? Read the review you chose with your teacher's permission by clicking the link at GrammarGalaxyBooks.com/RedStar.*

Review of Ferrari Land
Attraction Review: Ferrari Land
The Most Thrilling Theme Park: Ferrari Land
Ferrari Land Review: Families and Formula One Fans Can Live the Brand
Hold Tight for a 112mph Rollercoaster Ride in Ferrari Land
Race Simulator Rides Rev Up the Action at Spain's Ferrari Land

⭐ Step 3: Brainstorm Titles for the Places You've Described

Using one location you've written about in previous missions, *brainstorm title ideas for your description. Highlight your favorite.* **Note:** *Keep in mind the keywords people are searching online.*

Write a title that's a question.

_____

Use a sensory image from your writing as a title.

_____

Write a title beginning with an -ing verb.

_____

Write a one- or two-word title.

_____

Write a three-word title.

_____

Write a four-word title.

_____

Write a five-word title.

_____

Use a common saying or quote as a title.

_____

Change one word in the title above.

_____

Put two of the above titles together with a colon.

_____

Vocabulary Victory! Do you remember what these words mean? *Check Step 1 if you need a reminder.*

earnestly	"No, and we wanted to talk to you about it," Ellen said **earnestly**.
compelling	The review title is not very **compelling**.
negligence	This latest problem is a result of your **negligence**.

☆ Advanced Guardians Only

Ask for title advice. *Show your titles to your friends and see which title would make them want to read your place description. With your teacher's help, you may want to ask for opinions online. Many social media platforms have a poll feature you could use. When the votes are in, choose a title and share your place description. Check GrammarGalaxyBooks.com/RedStar for the link to the Grammar Guardians group for sharing.*

Speaking of sharing, please help us choose a title for our review of Movie Adventureland. Highlight your favorite.

Have You Ever Wanted to Be in the Movies?
A Screaming Good Time for Kids at Movie Adventureland
Experiencing a Dream Family Vacation at Movie Adventureland
Movie Adventureland
Movie Adventureland Review
Movie Adventureland Delivers Fun
A Kid's Dream Come True
I'll Be Back
We'll Be Back
We'll Be Back: Movie Adventureland Review

OFFICIAL GUARDIAN MAIL

Mission 31: Update

Dear guardians,

    Your titles are so creative! We love them and we are grateful for your help in choosing a title for our review. We know that our website will have a lot more readers as a result.

    Keep using the title prompts for creating titles and doing keyword research.

    We are including the solutions to the On Guard section.

Sincerely,

Kirk, Luke, and Ellen English

Guardians of Grammar Galaxy

<u>Step 1 Solutions</u>

On Guard.

1. **Name one way of successfully writing with a partner.** Agree on a meeting schedule; write separately, without concern for what your writing partner will think; edit together, write with one voice.

2. **Name one type of sentence starter.** Adverb, paired adjectives, prepositional phrase, transition words, subordinating conjunction, participle, article, subject.

3. **What are the five senses used in descriptive writing?** Sight, sound, taste, smell, touch.

4. **What is one way of organizing your descriptive writing?** Chronologically, importance, location.

5. **What is the most important part of a business letter?** Information so the recipient understands who you are and what you want.

Mission 32: Advice Column

Dear guardians,

    We received a request for advice from a reader who is frustrated with her younger brother. Ellen was ready to send her advice that wasn't the best. Our mother taught us how we could write a better response, and she had an idea. She suggested we start an advice column that you can help us write!

    Complete this mission and you'll be not only a guardian but an advice columnist. We are including the letter asking for advice and the information on advice columns from *The Guidebook to Grammar Galaxy*.

Sincerely,

Kirk, Luke, and Ellen English

Guardians of Grammar Galaxy

Dear Guardians,

    I know this isn't English related, but I thought you might be able to help me. I have a younger brother who annoys me all the time. When I start to play a video game, he wants a turn right then. He won't leave me alone when I have a friend over. And he is always making fun of me. What can I do?

Signed,

Frustrated Sister

Advice Column

Advice columns were traditionally published in newspapers and magazines. But they are now a part of a variety of digital media. A usually anonymous reader submits a question about a problem, hoping for advice from the columnist. Advice columnists are referred to as agony aunts and uncles in British English.

Columnists may have an area of expertise, such as medicine or psychology. They may write under a pseudonym or fictitious name. The columnist may actually be a group of writers writing under the same name.

Advice columnists follow these steps to write an effective column:
- **Decide who your audience is.** Consider age, gender, and specific life circumstances. You should have experience or education in answering your audience's questions.
- **Review other advice columns for your audience**. Determine how long and detailed your answers should be.
- **Restate the question.** After beginning with your reader's question, summarize the issue in a sentence. Make sure you also communicate empathy with your reader. For example, "Dealing with a bully can be really hard."
- **Don't lecture.** Your reader may have already made mistakes in trying to solve the problem. Focus on what is to be done going forward.
- **Focus on solving one problem.** Your reader may have numerous questions. Focus on the biggest issue that you can help with.
- **Provide multiple perspectives on the issue.** Consider the needs and feelings of each of the people involved in your reader's problem. To do that, you may need to ask other people for their advice. You may also need to research the best advice for this particular problem. Read your advice to friends and family before publishing it. Even if you are an expert, advise your reader to seek professional help when that's wise. You can't give the best advice when you don't know much about your reader.
- **Write casually.** Read your writing out loud to make sure it sounds natural. You want your reader to easily understand your advice, so avoid jargon.
- **Choose a title that grabs attention.** You want others with the same problem to want to read your article. "Boy Needs Help Convincing Parents to Get Dog" is more engaging than "Parents and Pet Ownership."
- **Proofread your response.** If your answer has grammar and spelling errors, your reader may not respect your advice.
- **Encourage readers to ask questions.** Give your readers a way to contact you to ask questions. If you receive questions apart from your advice column, make sure you get permission to publish the question. Keep the identity of your readers private.

☆ Step 1: On Guard & Review Advice

On Guard. *Highlight TRUE or FALSE for each question.*

1. Creating the best title requires brainstorming.   TRUE   FALSE

2. When writing with a partner, you should carefully consider what your partner will think.   TRUE   FALSE

3. Participles should <u>not</u> be used as sentence starters.   TRUE   FALSE

4. Descriptions should always be organized chronologically.   TRUE   FALSE

5. You should do some research to learn who is in charge of the department your business letter is addressed to.   TRUE   FALSE

Say each of these words in a sentence. *Examples are given.*

solemnly – seriously	My friend **solemnly** pledged to keep my secret.
retorted – answered	"I'm not a little kid," my sister **retorted**.
scoffed – made fun of	I **scoffed** when my brother said he was rich.

Review advice. *We looked up advice on dealing with a problem sibling. These are eight suggestions we found. Read Frustrated Sister's letter to a sibling, parent, and friend. Ask them which three pieces of advice are best for her. Then highlight your top three choices.*

1. Lock your bedroom door.
2. Play a trick to get your sibling away from you.
3. Make a deal with your sibling.
4. Play with your sibling.
5. Get help from parents.
6. Hide the game system.
7. Make fun of your sibling, so he leaves you alone.
8. Ignore the bad behavior.

⭐ <u>Step 2: Write Your Own Letter, Asking for Advice</u>

We need more letters for our advice column. Write a short letter, asking us for advice. Briefly explain the problem and sign the letter with an anonymous name.

Dear Kirk, Luke, and Ellen,

_____

_____

_____

_____

_____

_____

_____

_____

_____

_____

_____

Signed,

_____

Activity. *With your teacher's permission, read the advice given to to a girl about bedtime (find the link at GrammarGalaxyBooks.com/RedStar). Was this good advice? Do you have different advice for her?*

⭐ Step 3: Write an Advice Column

Answer the letter below with an advice column. *Use the outline below for your first draft. Then type it and proofread it.*

Dear Guardians,

I have a jealous friend. He doesn't want me to spend time with another friend in my neighborhood. When the other kid is at my house, my jealous friend will call and ask me to come to his house. He won't invite my other friend. What do I do?

Fought-Over Friend

Title_____

Restate problem _____

_____

Advice #1_____

_____

Advice #2_____

_____

Advice #3_____

_____

Signed,

_____

Vocabulary Victory! Do you remember what these words mean? *Check Step 1 if you need a reminder.*

solemnly	"There's just one problem," Ellen said **solemnly**.
retorted	"He makes fun of her, so it's only fair," Ellen **retorted**.
scoffed	"You thought putting a No Boys Allowed sign up would work?" Luke **scoffed**.

☆ <u>Advanced Guardians Only</u>

Turn your advice into a video. *You might make the letter from Step 3 visible in your video as you read it. Then give your advice.*

Mission 32: Update

Dear guardians of Grammar Galaxy,

We had a problem responding to a request for advice from one of our readers. We didn't know how to write good advice. Our mother taught us the basics from *The Guidebook to Grammar Galaxy*, but you taught us so much with the advice you wrote.

We now have an advice column for guardians by guardians. We would love to have you continue to write advice for our readers. And please let us know if you have a question you'd like answered. You can write us at grammargalaxybooks@gmail.com.

We are including the On Guard solutions.

Sincerely,

Kirk, Luke, and Ellen English

Guardians and Advice Columnists of Grammar Galaxy

<u>Step 1 Solutions</u>

On Guard.

1. Creating the best title requires brainstorming.   TRUE   FALSE

2. When writing with a partner, you should carefully consider what your partner will think.   TRUE   FALSE

3. Participles should <u>not</u> be used as sentence starters.   TRUE   FALSE

4. Descriptions should always be organized chronologically.   TRUE   FALSE

5. You should do some research to learn who is in charge of the department your business letter is addressed to.   TRUE   FALSE

Mission 33: Choosing a Research Paper Topic

Dear guardians,

Kirk has been asked to write a paper for the *Galactic Robotics Journal*. He is happy for the opportunity, but he was having a hard time choosing a topic. Father taught all of us how to choose a good research paper topic, and now he wants us to teach you.

We thought it would be good practice for all of us to write a research paper. We can add completed papers to our Grammar Galaxy Kids website. But first you have to research topics. Complete this mission and you'll have one! We're including information from *The Guide to Grammar Galaxy* to help you.

Sincerely,

Kirk, Luke, and Ellen English
Guardians of Grammar Galaxy

How to Choose a Research Paper Topic

To find the right research paper topic, do some library research. An encyclopedia or reference book can give you some ideas. When you find one, ask yourself if the topic:

- **interests you.** If it bores you, you won't write a good paper. It's also likely that your audience will be bored too.

- **is somewhat familiar.** You can write about a completely new topic. But you'll have less work if you already know something about the subject.

- **is appropriate for the audience.** Does it match the guidelines your teacher or publication has given you? Will your reader be able to understand it?

- **has enough written about it and not too much.** Search the library's catalog for books on the subject. Ask your teacher's or librarian's help in finding more resources in the library and online.

A topic like space with too much written about it is too broad. Choose a specific part of the topic like the planet Saturn to write about. A topic with few references is too narrow. You will have difficulty writing a paper of 3-5 pages. Expand the topic or choose another.

- **is better than another topic you find.** Be willing to change topics if you find one more interesting, familiar, appropriate, or with more sources.

After considering potential topics, be willing to choose a good topic rather than a perfect one. Perfectionism can keep you from getting started on your research paper.

☆ Step 1: On Guard & Library Research

On Guard. *Highlight the correct answer for each question.*

1. Advice columnists should:
   lecture   focus on one question   write formally

2. A good title always:
   interests readers   is mysterious   is your first idea

3. When writing with a partner:
   use one voice   edit separately   miss meetings

4. An interesting sentence starter is:
   an article   the subject   an adverb

5. Descriptive writing can be organized by:
   the alphabet   color   importance

Say each of these words in a sentence. *Examples are given.*

bestowed – given	My old princess crown was **bestowed** upon my sister.
diligent – hardworking	I haven't been as **diligent** as I could be in cleaning the bathroom.
potential – possible	I am making a list of **potential** gifts for my birthday wish list.

Library research. *Visit the library. Begin by choosing an encyclopedia or a reference book to look up robotics, horses, video games or another topic of your choice. Write down five potential subtopics you find interesting.*

1._____

2._____

3._____

4._____

5._____

⭐ Step 2: Evaluate Subtopics

Rate the subtopics you chose on each criterion to give it a score.
Rewrite the subtopics from Step 1 in the lines below. Then highlight 1-5 (5 being the highest score) for each criterion. Add the total score for each subtopic.

1._____
Interests you   1 2 3 4 5
Familiar   1 2 3 4 5
Good topic for kids 1 2 3 4 5   Total_____

2._____
Interests you   1 2 3 4 5
Familiar   1 2 3 4 5
Good topic for kids 1 2 3 4 5   Total_____

3._____
Interests you   1 2 3 4 5
Familiar   1 2 3 4 5
Good topicfor kids   1 2 3 4 5   Total_____

4._____
Interests you   1 2 3 4 5
Familiar   1 2 3 4 5
Good topic for kids 1 2 3 4 5   Total_____

5._____
Interests you   1 2 3 4 5
Familiar   1 2 3 4 5
Good topic for kids 1 2 3 4 5   Total_____

Activity. *Look for a fiction book to read on the topic of your choice.*

☆ Step 3: Look for Library Materials on Your Subtopic
Determine if your library has the right amount of material for your top-rated subtopics. *Do a library catalog search for books or articles on your top two subtopics from Step 2. Visit the library and find three books for each subtopic on the shelves. Then answer the questions below.*

Subtopic #1_____
Are there at least three sources on this subtopic?   Y N
Are any of the sources you found written for kids?   Y N
Are there no more than 10 kids' sources on this subtopic? Y N

Subtopic #1_____
Are there at least three sources on this subtopic?   Y N
Are any of the books you found written for kids?   Y N
Are there no more than 10 kids' sources on this subtopic? Y N

Circle the subtopic with the most yes answers. If they're tied, choose the subtopic with the sources that are easiest for you to read.

Vocabulary Victory! Do you remember what these words mean? *Check Step 1 if you need a reminder.*

bestowed	the conversation was all about the honor **bestowed** upon Kirk.
diligent	The queen smiled, proud of her **diligent** son.
potential	He thought about **potential** topics, but nothing seemed like the perfect one for him.

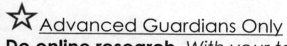 <u>Advanced Guardians Only</u>

Do online research. *With your teacher's help, look for kids' websites with information on your top two subtopics. Choose the subtopic that has one to three kid-friendly websites (and no more than ten) with the information you need.*

Mission 33: Update

Dear guardians and star researchers,

We love your topics and we can't wait to read your finished papers. Kirk is especially relieved to have a topic. He'll be writing about robot pets.

We are including the solutions to the On Guard section.

Sincerely,

Kirk, Luke, and Ellen English
Guardians of Grammar Galaxy

Step 1 Solutions

On Guard.

1. Advice columnists should:
   lecture   focus on one question   write formally

2. A good title always:
   interests readers   is mysterious   is your first idea

3. When writing with a partner:
   use one voice   edit separately   miss meetings

4. An interesting sentence starter is:
   an article   the subject   an adverb

5. Descriptive writing can be organized by:
   the alphabet   color   importance

Mission 34: Note-Taking & Outlining

Dear guardian friends,

Are you feeling like we're feeling? Are you overwhelmed with information for your research paper?

Our mother taught us that good note-taking and an outline can help. That's what we're asking you to do for this mission. You'll take notes from the books and articles you've found. Then you'll make an outline of the information, which Mother says will make writing the paper much faster. That sounds good to us! We hope it does to you too.

We're including the guidebook information on note-taking and outlining to help you complete your mission.

Sincerely,

Kirk, Luke, and Ellen English
Guardians of Grammar Galaxy

Taking Notes for a Research Paper

Before taking notes for a research paper, decide the three to five main points your paper will make.

To make this decision, skim the reference material you've collected. Write down the main topics covered in each, which are typically in bold or subheadings. Choose the most important and interesting topics. You may need to combine topics.

For example, in researching the giant panda, you may find information about:
– habitat
– diet
– teeth
– weight/size
– speed
– population
– how pandas are being protected
– relatives
– species
– behavior
– babies' growth

To limit your paper to three to five topics with enough material, you may create a main point called General Information. Under General Information, you may include information about the size, species, and habitat of pandas. Your second point might be called Life of Pandas. You can include information about growth of baby pandas, diet, as well as behavior of adults. Your third point could be Protecting Pandas. Here you can discuss population, threats, and how the Giant Panda is being protected.

When taking notes, you'll ignore information that doesn't add to the main points you'll be writing about. With your Giant Panda paper, you won't take notes on their teeth, speed, or relatives.

The two most common ways of taking notes are using note cards or a digital note-taking program. Both methods require you to use the following steps to take good notes.

1) Write down detailed information about the sources you are using. Include author name, book/article title, the name of the magazine or newspaper, or website URL. Include the publisher and place and date of publication if known. In the case of printed works, also write the location of the source (e.g., library). This will be helpful if you need to return to it. Number each source card so you can save time writing the number with your notes, rather than the source title.

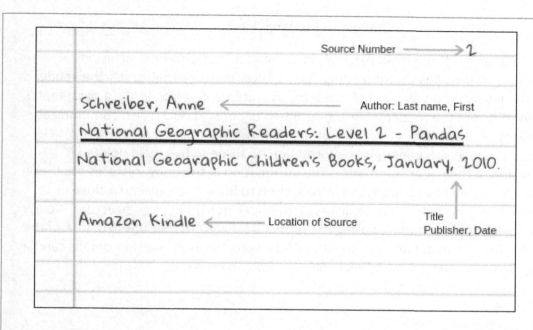

Source Number ⟶ 2

Schreiber, Anne ⟵——————— Author: Last name, First

National Geographic Readers: Level 2 - Pandas

National Geographic Children's Books, January, 2010.

Amazon Kindle ⟵——— Location of Source   Title
Publisher, Date

2) Add ONE fact or idea to each note, using abbreviations, keywords, or drawings. Your note should include:
   – the source card number
   – the order of the note, using letters (the second card from source 1 would be labeled 1B)
   – the subject of the note, including the main point it will support
   – the fact or information (being careful to include quotation marks if taken word for word from the source)
   – the page number on which the information was found if any.

2C

General Information: Habitat

Pandas live in 6 forests in the mountains of China.

p. 8

Outlining a Research Paper

A research paper has three main parts: an introduction, body, and a conclusion.

The introduction includes an interesting fact, quote, or story that grabs the reader's attention. The introduction also includes the thesis statement, which is like a paragraph's topic sentence. It tells the reader what the research paper is about. It also communicates the main points of the paper.

The body of the research paper gives information on three to five main points.

The conclusion of the paper summarizes the information in the body, restates the thesis in a new way, and may refer back to the introduction to bring the paper to a close.

An outline helps you to organize your research paper notes into this structure. Nearly any research paper can be outlined using the format below. Note that the structure of the outline moves from Roman numerals to capital letters to numbers. Further details can be added using lowercase letters and then lowercase Roman numerals.

   I. Introduction
     A. Interesting fact, quote, story
     B. Thesis statement
     C. Main points of paper

  II. Body
     A. Main point #1
       1. Fact or detail #1
       2. Fact or detail #2
       3. Fact or detail #3
     B. Main point #2
       1. Fact or detail #1
       2. Fact or detail #2
       3. Fact or detail #3
     C. Main point #3
       1. Fact or detail #1
       2. Fact or detail #2
       3. Fact or detail #3

 III. Conclusion
     A. Summary of Body
     B. Restatement of thesis
     C. Refer back to introduction

⭐ <u>Step 1: On Guard & Decide Your Three Main Points</u>

On Guard. *Answer the following questions or answer verbally for your teacher.*

1. What are three things to consider when choosing a research paper topic?

2. What are three ways to write an effective advice column?

3. What are three prompts for creating a good title?

4. What kinds of things should you say to your writing partner about his/her work?

5. What is your favorite interesting way of starting a sentence?

Say each of these words in a sentence. *Examples are given.*

unmoved – unaffected	My dog was **unmoved** when my brother pulled its ears.
sardonic – mocking	My mom says I'm not allowed to use a **sardonic** tone.
justifying – defending	Mom says there's no use **justifying** my failure to take out the trash.

Decide your three main points. *Skim the headings and subheadings of your research paper sources and list them below. Then write the three points that you will discuss in your paper. These should be the most important or interesting topics.* **Note:** *One of your main points may be a combination of a number of topics you've listed below.*

_____

_____

_____

_____

_____

_____

_____

_____

_____

_____

My research paper's main points are:

1._____

2._____

3._____

⭐ <u>Step 2: Take Notes</u>

Using note cards or a digital note card option at GrammarGalaxyBooks.com/Red Star, take notes from your sources. *First, create your source cards as described in The Guidebook to Grammar Galaxy. Then write one fact per card, including the source and which main point that fact supports. If you don't write the fact in your own words, use quotes around it.* **Note:** <u>Write the page number where you found the information, if any.</u>

⭐ Step 3: Create an Outline

Using your note cards, complete the outline below or create a digital outline using the document or note-taking program you used in step 2. *Use the extra lines for supporting facts only if needed.*

I. Introduction

  A. Interesting fact, quote, or story

_____

  B. Thesis statement and three main points

_____

II. Body

  A. Main point #1_____

    1. Supporting fact #1_____

    2. Supporting fact #2_____

    3. Supporting fact #3_____

_____

_____

  B. Main point #2_____

    1. Supporting fact #1_____

    2. Supporting fact #2_____

    3. Supporting fact #3_____

_____

_____

  C. Main point #3_____

    1. Supporting fact #1_____

    2. Supporting fact #2_____

    3. Supporting fact #3_____

_____

_____

III. Conclusion

    A. Summary of main points

    B. Reference to introduction_____

Vocabulary Victory! Do you remember what these words mean? *Check Step 1 if you need a reminder.*

unmoved	"Oh, hi, Father. I'm working on my research paper," he said **unmoved**.
sardonic	"You are," the king said in **sardonic** tone.
justifying	"Yes! For real!" Luke said, **justifying** himself.

⭐ <u>Advanced Guardians Only</u>

Get a head start on your research paper. *Put your note cards in order according to your outline. Then type a first draft of your research paper. Be sure to save it so you can find it.*

OFFICIAL GUARDIAN MAIL

Mission 34: Update

Dear guardians,

We have our outlines done, and we're happy to see that you worked hard to finish yours too. Mother was so impressed! If you haven't written your first draft yet, it shouldn't take that long. You'll simply write the introduction, body, and conclusion with your outline in front of you. You'll include the information from your note cards for each section. Mother says we should tell you that you may decide not to use every card.

We don't want to keep you from writing your paper, so we will just have you check your On Guard answers against the solutions we're including.

Sincerely,

Kirk, Luke, and Ellen English

Guardians of Grammar Galaxy

<u>Step 1 Solutions</u>

On Guard.

1. **What are three things to consider when choosing a research paper topic?** Interests you, somewhat familiar, has enough written about it but not too much, is appropriate for the audience, is better than another topic you found.

2. **What are three ways to write an effective advice column?** Decide who your audience is, review other advice columns for your audience, restate the question, don't lecture, focus on solving one problem, provide multiple perspectives, write casually, choose an attention-grabbing title, proofread your response, encourage readers to ask questions.

3. **What are three prompts for creating a good title?** Write a title that's a question; use a sensory image from your writing; begin with an -ing verb; write one to five word titles; use a common saying or quote; change a word in a common saying or quote; put titles together with a colon.

4. **What kinds of things should you say to your writing partner about his/her work?** I noticed; I felt; I pictured; Say more about…; Can you explain…?

5. **What is your favorite interesting way of starting a sentence?** Adverb, preposition, participle, paired adjectives, transition words, subordinating conjunction.

Mission 35: Citing References

Dear guardians,

Have you ever seen a Style Guide show on planet Composition? We hadn't either. But we've learned that it's important to know what's fashionable for citing references in your research papers.

It can be a bit confusing, so we are sending you a mission to make it clear. We are fortunate to have digital tools that will format our sources for us (Queen).

The reference in the sentence above is from our personal interview with our mother, written in MLA format. If we were including the interview on a Works Cited page, it would look like this:

Queen, The. Personal interview. 25 April, 3000.

Fortunately, you don't have to memorize how to format every type of source. You'll use one or more of the digital tools found at GrammarGalaxyBooks.com/RedStar to format your research paper in MLA format.

We're including information on citing sources from the guidebook to help you.

Sincerely,

Kirk, Luke, and Ellen English

Guardians of Grammar Galaxy

Citing References

Information in a paper that comes from a reference such as a book, magazine, newspaper, website, or another source must be cited or credited. An exception to citations is when information is common knowledge that is presented in numerous sources. A second exception is when you are summarizing previously cited information. When in doubt, cite the reference.

There are two places references are listed in a paper: 1) in the text with the information from that source; and 2) in a list at the end of a paper. References listed in the text must appear in the final list, and references at the end of the paper should appear in the text.

The way references are cited is determined by the style guide used. Your teacher or publication may give you the style to use. MLA (Modern Language Association) is most commonly used for language arts and cultural studies. APA (American Psychological Association) is most commonly used for psychology, education, and the sciences. Chicago (Chicago Manual of Style) is used most often for business, history, and fine arts. See the following chart for the main differences in style. However, note that style guides are always being updated. Check a recent style guide or use a digital tool to correctly format sources in your list.

☆ Step 1: On Guard & Prepare Your Paper

On Guard. *Answer the following questions or answer verbally for your teacher.*

1. How can you decide the three to five main points your research paper will make?

2. What attitude can keep you from choosing a good research paper topic?

3. How can you provide multiple perspectives on a reader's problem for an advice column?

4. How can you make sure a title you choose has good SEO?

5. Why is it important to have one writing partner add personal touches to your joint writing?

Say each of these words in a sentence. *Examples are given.*

enthralling – fascinating	The documentary about the rock climber was **enthralling**.
stunned – shocked	When I found out I won the giveaway, I was **stunned**.
therapeutic – healing	My mother says honey is **therapeutic**.

Prepare your paper. *Type a first draft of your research paper if you haven't already. Proofread your paper. Check the boxes below after you've made sure your paper has these qualities. Save any changes you make.*

☐ Each sentence begins with a capital letter and ends with an end mark.

☐ Sentences begin with various sentence starters.

☐ Proper nouns are capitalized, and common nouns are not.

☐ There are no run-on sentences (commas alone aren't used to separate complete sentences).

☐ Transition words (first, next, also) are used to introduce new topics.

☐ A good title has been chosen.

☐ Any spelling or grammar errors highlighted by your document program have been corrected.

☐ An MLA header with page numbers has been created. See GrammarGalaxyBooks.com/RedStar for instructions.

☐ An MLA title page has been created. See example below. Use Grammar Guardians for "Instructor" and Red Star for "Course."

Ellen English
Grammar Guardians
Red Star
May 5, 2021

The Lipizzan: Horse of Royalty

⭐ Step 2: Add In-Text Citations

For each note card fact or quote that you've included in your paper, add an in-text MLA citation for the source card. *For information that is common knowledge, such as "The giant panda is found in south China," no citation is needed. However, if you aren't sure if a citation is needed, use one. For books or articles that have an author and page numbers, the MLA format is (Author Last Name, page number). For all other source types, use a citation generator linked at GrammarGalaxyBooks.com/ RedStar to create a correct in-text citation.*

⭐ Step 3: Create a Works Cited Page

Use one of the citation generators listed at GrammarGalaxyBooks.com/RedStar to create a Works Cited page. *You will have to copy and paste the citations to your research paper document. The Works Cited page will be the last numbered page of your research paper. "Works Cited" will be centered at the top of the page. Authors or source titles will be listed alphabetically followed by a period. See the example below.*

Jones 7

Works Cited

Arnold, Caroline, and Richard Hewett. Panda. Morrow Junior Books, 1992.

Bradford, Alina. "Giant Pandas: Facts About the Charismatic Black and White

Bears." LiveScience, Purch, 15 Mar. 2019, www.livescience.com/27335-

giant-pandas.html.

"Giant Panda." National Geographic, 21 Sept. 2018,

www.nationalgeographic.com/animals/mammals/g/giant-panda/.

Greve, Tom. Giant Pandas. Rourke Pub., 2011.

Vocabulary Victory! Do you remember what these words mean? *Check Step 1 if you need a reminder.*

enthralling	Your research paper on robotic pets is **enthralling**!
stunned	He was **stunned** by what he'd read.
therapeutic	That's my source for what I wrote about **therapeutic** pets.

 Advanced Guardians Only

Format your Works Cited page correctly. *The source list should be double spaced. All lines of the source after the first should be indented half an inch. Watch a video link for instructions for your document program at GrammarGalaxyBooks.com/RedStar. Have your teacher review your completed paper.*

Mission 35: Update

Dear guardians,

You have great style! The references you cited are formatted in just the right way. We learned that our mother was right. Digital tools do make formatting our references much easier!

Your research papers are enthralling. We hope you learned a lot and had fun writing them. Kirk's paper was accepted by the *Galactic Robotics Journal*. We won't be surprised if your papers are accepted for publication too.

We are including the solutions for the On Guard section.

Sincerely,

Kirk, Luke, and Ellen English

Guardians of Grammar Galaxy

<u>Step 1 Solutions</u>

On Guard.

1. **How can you decide the three to five main points your research paper will make?** Write down the main topics covered in each, which are typically in bold or subheadings. Choose the most important and interesting topics. You may need to combine topics.

2. **What attitude can keep you from choosing a good research paper topic?** Perfectionism.

3. **How can you provide multiple perspectives on a reader's problem for an advice column?** Ask friends and family for their advice.

4. **How can you make sure a title you choose has good SEO?** Search the topic online.

5. **Why is it important to have one writing partner add personal touches to your joint writing?** It makes the writing seem like it was written by one author.

Mission 36: Informative Speaking

Dear guardians,

    This mission is Father's order. He wants all of us to know how to give an informative speech. It all started because Kirk thought he could just read his paper at the Galactic Robotics Conference. Father said that would be too boring.

    After we learned how to give a good informative speech, I (Ellen) had the idea that we could give our speeches in our Grammar Girls and Guys groups. We know we can learn a lot from your speeches. Kirk is working hard on his right now. Please complete this mission as soon as possible.

Sincerely,

Luke and Ellen English

Guardians of Grammar Galaxy

P.S. We are including the Informative Speaking article from *The Guidebook to Grammar Galaxy*.

Informative Speaking

A good informative speech begins with a clear outline. Your speech will have an introduction, body, and conclusion.

In most cases, you will want to outline the body of your speech first. Begin by deciding on the three to five main subtopics you will speak about. Under each subtopic, note the key information you will share. Next, plan how to hold your audience's attention for each subtopic. Some common attention-getters to consider are **anecdotes**, jokes, photos, graphs, and demonstrations. Your audience is more likely to remember your attention-getter than your words.

Next, outline your speech's introduction. Begin with an attention-getter that helps your audience understand why your information is important to them. A funny or emotional statistic, quote, or story is a good option. Follow your attention-getter by telling your audience your authority to speak on the subject, even if that's just an interest in the topic. Finally, tell your audience the subtopics you'll be covering in your speech.

The last step in outlining your speech is writing the conclusion. First, you'll review the information you've covered. Then you'll encourage your audience by referring back to your first attention-getter.

See the sample partial outline for a speech on puppy training.

You will cite fewer references in an informative speech. When you do use references for statistics, quotes, or unique ideas, you will give less detail. For example, you might say, "According to the American Kennel Club website, the most important part of puppy training is to start early." Or you might say, "According to a 2013 issue of the *Journal of Veterinary Medical Science*, puppy training is the key to shaping a dog's future behavior."

☆ Step 1: On Guard & Rewrite Your Research Paper Outline

On Guard. *Highlight the correct answer for each question.*

1. References are listed:
   in the text   in your diary   on notecards only

2. How many facts should be listed per notecard?
   one   two   three

3. Writing a research paper is easier if the topic is:
   very narrow   very broad   familiar

4. Before writing an advice column, know your:
   shoe size   audience   hair color

5. To come up with a good title, try different:
   audiences   citation styles   word lengths

Say each of these words in a sentence. *Examples are given.*

dampen – reduce	Bad reviews didn't **dampen** my enthusiasm about the new movie.
landscaping – yard design	My dad says the neighbor could use some **landscaping** help.
anecdotes – stories	Grandpa tells me the same **anecdotes** every time I see him.

Rewrite your research paper outline. *Refer to your research paper outline from Mission 34. Write a new outline below with your three main points. Add your authority to speak on the subject. Limit the supporting facts for each main point to the three most interesting for your audience.*

I. Introduction

  A. Interesting fact, quote, or story (Why should your audience care?)

  B. Authority to speak on the topic (Interest, experience)

  C. Three main points you'll be discussing

II. Body

  A. Main point #1_____

    1. Supporting fact #1_____

    2. Supporting fact #2_____

    3. Supporting fact #3_____

  B. Main point #2_____

    1. Supporting fact #1_____

    2. Supporting fact #2_____

    3. Supporting fact #3_____

  C. Main point #3_____

    1. Supporting fact #1_____

    2. Supporting fact #2_____

    3. Supporting fact #3_____

III. Conclusion

  A. Summary of main points

  B. Reference to introduction_____

⭐ Step 2: Plan Attention Getters

Rewrite the body of your outline from Step 1. *Then write how you will get your audience's attention for each main point. Do you have an anecdote, a joke, or an interesting statistic? Make note of your attention-getters where you will use them in our outline below.* **Note:** *You may have an attention-getter for some supporting facts but not others. Include at least one for every main point.*

A. Main point #1_____

   1. Supporting fact #1_____

   2. Supporting fact #2_____

   3. Supporting fact #3_____

B. Main point #2_____

   1. Supporting fact #1_____

   2. Supporting fact #2_____

   3. Supporting fact #3_____

C. Main point #3_____

   1. Supporting fact #1_____

   2. Supporting fact #2_____

   3. Supporting fact #3_____

Activity. *Do more research, if needed, to look for attention-getters for your speech.*

⭐ Step 3: Practice Giving Your Speech with Your Outline

Using only your outline, give your speech. *Before practicing, type your speech outline from Step 2, but include the Introduction and Conclusion from Step 1. Your completed outline should fit on one page. Practice numerous times until you feel confident and you are speaking smoothly. Then video record your speech. If you aren't looking up from your paper, aren't using any gestures, or you're using too many gestures, practice some more. Then video record again.*

Advanced Guardians, complete the mission on the next page. All other guardians, give your prepared speech to your family, class, or co-op.

Vocabulary Victory! Do you remember what these words mean? *Check Step 1 if you need a reminder.*

dampen	She didn't say anything to **dampen** his enthusiasm.
landscaping	You need to know how to do **landscaping**.
anecdotes	Some common attention-getters to consider are **anecdotes** and jokes.

⭐ <u>Advanced Guardians Only</u>

Create a slide presentation or visual aids to add to your speech.
Check GrammarGalaxyBooks.com/RedStar for slide options. Use minimal text per slide. Otherwise, your slides will be hard to read from a distance. Photos and graphs can add a lot of interest. Models and demonstrations make great visual aids. Once you've created your slides or props, practice using them. Then give your prepared speech to an audience.

398

Mission 36: Update

Dear guardian friends,

      Your speeches were anything but boring! I (Ellen) am so glad I had the idea of having you give speeches in your Grammar Girls and Guys groups. Even Luke enjoyed speaking about video games. Kirk was grateful for the opportunity to practice before speaking at the conference. Father heard many compliments on his speech. The audience was especially wowed by his demonstration of a robotic pet.

      We are sending you the On Guard solutions to this mission.

Sincerely,

Kirk, Luke, and Ellen English

Guardians of Grammar Galaxy

P.S. You are ready to take the final Red Star Challenge. You're leveling up! Review what you've learned in previous units before you take it.

<u>Step 1 Solutions</u>

On Guard.

1. References are listed:
   in the text   in your diary   on notecards only

2. How many facts should be listed per notecard?
   one   two   three

3. Writing a research paper is easier if the topic is:
   very narrow   very broad   familiar

4. Before writing an advice column, know your:
   shoe size   audience   hair color

5. To come up with a good title, try different:
   audiences   citation styles   word lengths

Red Star Final Challenge I

Carefully read all the possible answers and then *highlight the letter for the* **one** *best answer.*

1. **In writing an informative speech:**
   a. outline the body first
   b. write the title first
   c. write the introduction first

2. **Three reference style guides are:**
   a. FBI, CIA, and Minneapolis
   b. MLA, APA, and Chicago
   c. neither a nor b

3. **The following should be at the top of a business letter:**
   a. closing
   b. who you are and why you're writing
   c. name or company name and address

4. **I need the following from the store____**
   What punctuation mark belongs in the blank of this sentence?
   a. ,
   b. ;
   c. :

5. **After we had dinner we went to a movie.**
   Which form of the sentence is written correctly?
   a. After we had dinner, we went to a movie.
   b. After we had dinner; we went to a movie.
   c. After we had dinner. We went to a movie.

6. **Some of the flour _____ on the floor.**
   Which word belongs in the blank?
   a. is
   b. are
   c. were

7. *I'm getting popcorn for* ____ *and* ____.
   Which pronouns belong in the blanks above?
   a. she, I
   b. her, I
   c. her, me

8. **I don't know** _____ **she is going or not.**
   Which word belongs in the blank above?
   a. weather
   b. whether
   c. wether

9. **The purse left in the café is** _____.
   Which word belongs in the blank above?
   a. it's
   b. her's
   c. hers

10. **Darkness/night usually symbolizes:**
    a. danger
    b. peace
    c. power

Number Correct:_____/10

☆ *Advanced Guardian Vocabulary Challenge*

For an extra challenge, highlight the word that belongs in each blank.

1. **The price of soda at the theater is _____.**
   ruffled   impression   exorbitant

2. **My room doesn't have to be _____, just picked up.**
   pristine   demurely   protocol

3. **The wait before summer vacation seems _____.**
   conciliatory   interminable   postpone

4. **I plan to _____ for a higher allowance.**
   defiantly   lofted   negotiate

5. **The warm cookies were just too _____ for me.**
   compelling   retorted   negligence

6. **I _____ when my brother said he was rich.**
   scoffed   earnestly   solemnly

7. **My old princess crown was _____ upon my sister.**
   justifying   bestowed   diligent

8. **My mom says I'm not allowed to use a _____ tone.**
   unmoved   potential   sardonic

9. **The documentary about the rock climber was _____.**
   stunned   landscaping   enthralling

10. **Bad reviews didn't _____ my enthusiasm about the new movie.**
    dampen   therapeutic   anecdotes

Number Correct _____ / 10

Red Star Final Challenge 1 Answers
1.a; 2.b; 3.c; 4.c; 5.a; 6.a; 7.c; 8.b; 9.c; 10.a

If you got 9 or more correct, congratulations! You're now a Red Star guardian and you are ready for the Blue Star book. See GrammarGalaxyBooks.com/shop for ordering.

If you did not get 9 or more correct, don't worry. You have another chance. You may want to have your teacher review the information from each chapter on the questions you missed. Then take the Red Star Final Challenge 2. Remember to **choose the <u>one</u> best answer**.

Advanced Guardian Vocabulary Challenge Answers
1. exorbitant
2. pristine
3. interminable
4. negotiate
5. compelling
6. scoffed
7. bestowed
8. sardonic
9. enthralling
10. dampen

Red Star Final Challenge 2

Carefully read all the possible answers and then highlight the letter for the **one** best answer.

1. **The introduction of a research paper could include:**
   a. an interesting fact
   b. a quote
   c. either a or b

2. **In the conclusion of an informative speech:**
   a. review what you've said
   b. refer back to the introduction
   c. both a and b

3. **In the sentence <u>I hit myself with a hammer.</u>, *myself* is a:**
   a. reflexive pronoun
   b. a direct object
   c. both a and b

4. **The word <u>that</u> is a/an:**
   a. demonstrative pronoun
   b. interrogative pronoun
   c. reflexive pronoun

5. **In the sentence <u>It was the best of times.</u>, *times* is:**
   a. the direct object
   b. the indirect object
   c. the object of the preposition

6. **In the sentence <u>I don't like lying.</u>, *lying* is:**
   a. a participle
   b. a preposition
   c. neither a nor b

7. **Which of the following sentences is correct?**
   a. The girl grabbed 5 pencils.
   b. The girl grabbed five pencils.
   c. 5 pencils were grabbed by the girl.

8. **Which of the following sentences is correct?**
   a. She was going on a once-in-a-lifetime trip.
   b. She was going on a once in a lifetime trip.
   c. She-was-going-on-a-once-in-a-lifetime trip.

9. **Solve the analogy. bird:nest::king:_____**
   a. planet
   b. space
   c. castle

10. **Red Star guardians are the greatest minds of our time. is an example of:**
    a. hyperbole
    b. foreshadowing
    c. analogies

Number Correct:_____/10

Red Star Challenge 2 Answers
1.c; 2.c; 3.c; 4.a; 5.c; 6.a; 7.b; 8.a; 9.c; 10.a

If you got 9 or more correct, congratulations! You're now a Red Star guardian and you are ready for the Blue Star book. See GrammarGalaxyBooks.com/shop for ordering.

If you did not get 9 or more correct, don't worry. Review the questions you missed with your teacher. You may want to get more practice using the resources at GrammarGalaxyBooks.com/RedStar. Your teacher can ask you other questions like the ones you missed and if you get them correct, you'll be a Yellow Star guardian and you will be ready for the Blue Star book. See GrammarGalaxyBooks.com/shop for ordering.

Official Red Star Guardian

THIS CERTIFICATE IS TO ACKNOWLEDGE THE ACHIEVEMENTS OF

ON THIS _____ _____ DAY OF _____, 20 ___ .

Kirk, Luke, and Ellen English

GUARDIANS OF GRAMMAR GALAXY

Made in United States
Orlando, FL
07 July 2024

48673002R00226